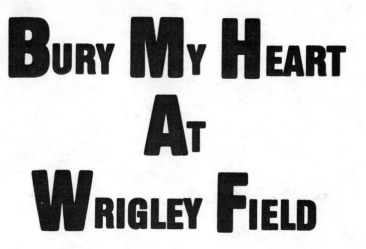

BURY MY HEART AT WRIGLEY FIELD

THE HISTORY OF THE

CHICAGO CUBS

WHEN THE CUBS WERE THE WHITE SOX
BY
LARRY D. NAMES

Sportsbook Publishing Co.
Neshkoro, Wisconsin
1990

Table of Contents

A summary of the development of the game of baseball through the 1860s. The first teams. The spread of the game. The first baseball organization. The first professionals.

Baseball in Chicago before the Cubs. The Excelsior Base Ball Club of Chicago. The baseball tournament of 1867. Lewis Meacham's editorial efforts to create a new team in Chicago.

Tom Foley and Lewis Meacham conspire to organize a new team for Chicago based on the example of the Cincinnati Red Stockings. The birth of the Cubs' organization as the Chicago Base Ball Club.

The first Cub player and captain Jimmy Wood. The first roster. The 1870 season. Winning the unofficial national title which is disputed by New York.

To my brother Chuck,
Thanks for making me a Cub fan!

Preface

The thrill of victory!

That's for Cub fans. Because from 1946 until 1984, victories were often far and few in between, so we learned to cherish each and every win. Oh, there were some glorious moments all right. Like 1969 when the Cubs rolled through the National League from April to mid–August; four magnificent months. Then the Mets forgot they were losers and began playing like the 1950s Yankees. The Cubs came up second; they may as well have been last. Cubs fans hung their heads in pain, humiliation. Egad! beaten out by the Mets. The shame of it all!

I cried. I admit it. I cried. I'm a Cub fan. I have emotions; I feel things deeply. Isn't that part of being a true Cubs fan? Isn't it part of the tradition? Isn't it?

That was a very good question that I asked myself a long time ago. Isn't being a Cubs fan proof that you're alive, that you feel for others? Isn't it traditional to cry for our Cubbies when they fold up in late summer almost every year? (Or so it seems they do anyway.)

No, that isn't the essence of being a Cubs fan. Although we can take defeat with grace, in our hearts we're winners. And our Cubs are winners, too. Or at least, they used to be. The history books say so, and my dad told me that they were winners when he was a kid. The books could be wrong but not Dad. He lived in Chicago and was a knotholer when Tinker was scooping up grounders and feeding them to Evers who relayed them to Chance for the most famous doubleplay combination in the annals of the game. He was there when the Cubs moved into Wrigley Field in 1916, then known as Weeghman Park. Naw, Dad wouldn't make up a story like that. The Cubs had to have been winners back then.

Of course, the Chicago Cubs were winners; not just once but 16 times they won the National League pennant from 1876 to 1945. They even won the World Series in 1907 and 1908. And when they weren't in the top spot, they were almost always fighting for the title. Or were they?

That was another fine question that I asked myself, and it led me into doing some deep research on the Cubs.

I started by reading a few books on the history of baseball because books on the history of the Cubs were rare — as in scarce and as in exceptional; there just aren't very many good books on the Cubs. A few that really deserve mentioning are: *The Golden Era Cubs* and *The New Era Cubs*, both by Eddie Gold and Art Ahrens; and *A.G. Spalding and the Rise of Baseball, The Promise of American Sport* by Peter Levine. The two-volume set by Gold and Ahrens isn't really a history of the Cubs as much as it is a collection of biographical sketches of many of the men who played significant parts in the history of the Cubs. They are excellent reading, and both are important books on our favorite subject. I treasure my copies. Levine's book on Spalding is very scholarly and may be a bit dry for some tastes, but its importance to the history of the Cubs cannot be depreciated by this very minor limitation. The author gave me a very real sense of the times and the man of which he was writing, and I found his book to be a great assistance in researching my own.

It was in the reading of these books and others that I found discrepancies on various points, and it was these disagreements on the facts that led me to turn to the men who lived during the era which I was studying. These men were the sportswriters of their day, and I sought them out in the pages of their newspapers which still live in the archives of several historical societies and libraries across this nation.* And when I read the words they wrote in yesteryears, I was quite amazed that so many modern authors had only skimmed the surface of history with their hardbound and paperback reports of how the game was played in the past. I was astounded at how much more there was to tell. When I related some of these facts to my good friend Dr. David Bills (a Pirate fan, but so what? — nobody's perfect), he listened politely, then diplomatically suggested in the kindest of words that I tell someone who cared, like another Cubs fan.

David was so right. All this knowledge I've gained about the Cubs shouldn't be locked up in my brain alone. That would be wrong, totally selfish. What to do? How do I tell my fellow Cubs fans that our team dates back to 1869 when it was but a gleam in the eye of one Tom

---

* *The Great Chicago Fire* of 1871 destroyed almost all of the newspaper buildings, offices, equipment, and early copies of nearly every publication in the city, making research of that time difficult but not impossible. Also destroyed were many private papers, especially those of the Chicago Base Ball Club.

Bury My Heart at Wrigley Field

Foley. Tom who?

See what I mean? Not one book — excuse me, there is one book that mentions Tom Foley: Macmillan's *The Baseball Encyclopedia*. But the authors of that enormous work are a bit confused about Foley. The name, dates, and places belong to the Tom Foley who should be credited with founding the Cubs back in 1869, but the playing statistics under his moniker belong to another Tom Foley, the real baseball player who hailed from Rockford, Illinois.

My heart was broken again when I read Jim Enright's history of the Cubs because he sort of glossed over the early years of the team, and of the few facts he did have, some were misleading or incorrect. But forget about those minor things because Mr. Enright wrote a great book. I suggest reading it for the sheer pleasure of enjoying the work of one of Chicago's all–time superstar sportswriters.

Facts like Foley's involvement in founding the Cubs and how William Ambrose Hulbert, the founder of the National League, manipulated the corporate strings of the Chicago Base Ball Association to take over the Cubs in 1876 pulled at my heart, and suddenly I felt like a kid who discovers at age 17 that he was adopted. I wanted to cry. Here I was, 39 years old, and I had been denied the truth about the birth of my team, our team, the Chicago Cubs, all these years. There was only one thing for me to do.

And here it is. I hope you like reading it as much as I loved researching and writing it.

Introduction

Mrs. O'Leary's cow allegedly kicked over a lantern, and most of Chicago burned to the ground. So the fable goes.

If it's true, Ol' Bossy might be forgiven because the Garden City, which was Chicago's nickname then, was already in need of a little urban renewal in 1871.

If that cow was guilty of arson, then Chicago baseball fans may never forgive the bovine for beginning the saddest tradition in all of sports history: the seemingly annual September swoon of the Chicago Cubs.

The Chicago White Stockings baseball club — the first of several nicknames by which the Chicago Cubs were known — was a member of the National Association (NA). The NA was a loose affiliation of professional baseball players that many historians refuse to accept as being a major league; but in 1871, it was the only professional organization around. It had the best players and the best attendance and offered the only thing resembling a pennant. To win the NA title was the ultimate in baseball that year, but Mrs. O'Leary's cow allegedly kept the Chicagoans from ending up on top with one swoop of a hoof.

The baseball season was almost at an end for '71 when *The Great Chicago Fire* destroyed the White Stockings' lakefront ball park, forcing the team to play its last three

13

games on the road instead of at home as originally scheduled. The White Stockings lost all three contests and slipped from atop the association's standings to finish in second place; and thus, the tradition of Chicago teams folding in late season was started.

Or so the story goes in other books.

While they did lose those last three games on the road, there was more to it than that, the full story of which is detailed later in this book.

Of course, the Cubs (or White Stockings, Whites, Colts, etc.) haven't always folded in the latter part of every season. There have been years when they were so bad that they were completely out of the pennant race by the 4th of July, and there have been campaigns when they were able to hang in until the last week. They've even won some pennants over the years. The Cubs were especially adept at winning it all in the early years of professional baseball's history. During the first decade plus one year of the National League (NL), the Chicago entry captured the pennant six times; at one point winning five out of seven years. From 1906 to 1910, they won four pennants and two World Series. They brought home top honors in the NL six more times from 1918 to 1945, then spent a score of years in the second division.

Of all the teams in Major League baseball, the Chicago Cubs have the longest history, dating back to 1869 when not everything was recorded for posterity's sake. The Cubs have played at more ball parks; had more ball-players, more managers, more coaches; played more games; scored more runs; won more games; and lost more games than any other club in the history of the game. Simply put, the Chicago Cubs of the National League are the oldest continuously operated baseball organization in history.

To say the Cincinnati Reds are the oldest team in baseball is an absolute mistake because they've only been in the NL since 1890 and were only in the American Association (AA) since 1882 before that. Porkopolis, as the Ohio city was known then, had no big league team or professional baseball club in 1881. Prior to that, the Star Club of Cincinnati of 1880 had moved there from Syracuse, N.Y., because the Cincinnati Club had folded up at the end of the 1879 season. Of course, everyone concedes the fact that the first *publicly announced all professional* baseball team was based in Cincinnati, but this club folded up in 1870.

Harry Wright, the captain and manager, of the Cincinnati team then moved to Boston and founded a new club and a new organization: the National Association of Professional Base Ball Players, the NA. Wright's nine was nicknamed the Red Stockings, the same as his Ohio team had been known. The club he helped to found remained active into the 20th century, being known later as the Bees and the Braves. In 1953, the Braves moved to Milwaukee, and in the next decade, they moved again, this time to Atlanta.

The Chicago Cubs were born in 1869 as a stock company known as the Chicago Base Ball Club. Because they wore white leggings as part of their first uniforms, they became known as the White Stockings during their first season of 1870 and continued to be called by this name for most of the next two decades, even when they didn't wear white socks. *The Great Chicago Fire* interrupted their playing for two years, 1872–73; but they returned to the field in 1874. The club, i.e., the organization that owned the team, did not cease to exist because of the fire; it continued to operate as a business through the years the team wasn't playing games on the field.

Bury My Heart at Wrigley Field

Because of this continuous operation of the original organization down through the years, the Chicago Cubs are the oldest team in baseball. The club was born in 1869, put its team on hold for two years, but survived into the next century and beyond. No other team or organization can make that claim.

In spite of this lengthy life, the Chicago Cubs have never had a definitive history written about them. Great statistical works have been compiled on the Cubs but no books telling their story. Of course, compiling numbers is the love of many baseball fans, but knowing that every hit wasn't a line drive or that every homer wasn't a rocket shot is the mark of the true baseball fan. The stories behind the numbers are the real history of the game. Few writers — Bill James being one exception with his *Baseball Abstracts* — have been able to give them their proper context. Whether the task was too great or too daring is unknown.

Very few comprehensive histories of Major League baseball teams have ever been written, and that is a shame. Several teams should have their histories written because so much has happened over the decades, on the field and off, that the box scores can never begin to tell their full stories.

If ever a team or organization deserved to be chronicled in detail for posterity, it is the Chicago Cubs.

The Cubs have come full circle from their beginnings in 1869 to the Dallas Green Era in the 1980s. The team was given impetus at birth by *The Chicago Tribune*, and 112 years later, it was given new life when the Tribune Company, the corporation that evolved from the *Tribune*, purchased the Cubs from the Wrigley family.

Joseph Medill, the publisher of the *Tribune* when the Cubs were born, was one of the first stockholders in the Chicago Base Ball Club and one of its earliest enthusiasts.

Through the *Tribune*, he threw his full editorial support behind the team, pumping life into it at time when Chicago was desperate for a winner. Medill's descendants, as the Tribune Company, gave the team new life in 1981 by hiring Dallas Green and by literally giving him a blank check with which to build Chicago a "new tradition" at a time when the Windy City was in dire need of one.

From Lewis Meacham and T.Z. Cowles, who wrote for the *Tribune* during the Cubs' earliest days, to Harry Caray, Steve Stone, Dwayne Staats, and Dave Nelson, the play–by–play announcers on WGN–TV and –Radio, the media of Chicago have played a dynamic role in the history of the Chicago franchise. Meacham's rah–rah ballyhooing of the early Cubs in the *Tribune* ignited the imaginations of young boys all over the Midwest to aspire to become professional baseball players for Chicago and encouraged fans throughout the region to turn out for games and make the team a financial success. The contagious enthusiasm of Harry Caray with the incisive analysis of Steve Stone on national cable TV telecasts of WGN and the adroit reporting of Dwayne Staats with the graphic interpretation of Dave Nelson on Cubs–Radio Network broadcasts carried by stations as far away from Chicago as Arizona and Florida made the Cubs America's team in the 1980s.

Medill, Meacham, and Cowles were journalists, and like most newspapermen of their time, they were prone to fits of sentiment in print. When their team won, they danced for joy on the pages of the *Tribune*; when the team lost, they cried buckets of ink. Their feelings carried over to the fans, touching their heartstrings, creating a familial bond between them and their team. This fan loyalty and emotion intensified over the years until it materialized in the 1980s as the Die–Hard Cubs Fan Club.

Bury My Heart at Wrigley Field

Because of their devotion to their team, Cubs fans deserve to be given a detailed historical perspective that preserves the traditions of baseball's oldest franchise. To meet this end, we must begin at the beginning.

1

B.C.
The National Game
Before the Cubs

Baseball is a most illogical sport. It's a game where the
defense has possession of the ball but gives the offense
the opportunity to score on each potential play. This is
not sensible, but this unique aspect of the game is only a
small portion of baseball's charm. Another part of its
charm is its history.

Exactly who invented baseball will never be known
because baseball has no definitive beginning, and hope—
fully, it won't ever have an end. It's not hard to imagine
some cave man picking up a stick in one hand and a rock in
the other and wondering how far he could hit the stone
with the club. Suffice it to say that the game most likely
evolved from such primitive origins.

Of course, as civilization marched forward, so did the
game until it eventually made an appearance in medieval
England where it became part of a contest known as "town
ball". This unique little sport was played by the folk of two
relatively close communities. The people of one town
would dare the citizens of the other to stop them from
rolling a ball from the center of the challenger's village

square to the middle of theirs. In some areas, the ball was made of a pig's or cow's bladder and was large enough to be kicked from town to town. In others, the ball was small and made of string covered with leather and the contestants batted it from town to town with sticks.

From this one game evolved football (soccer to Americans and Canadians) and a game called "rounders" because the idea was to strike a thrown ball with a stick then run *around* a group of bases, touching each one in passing and if the bases could be rounded safely (the word *safely* shouldn't be taken lightly here because a runner could be put out by being hit with the ball), a round was scored. This sport had its rule and name variations, including "stool ball" and, believe it or not, baseball.

"Stool ball" was being played in England as early as the 14th century. The modern moniker for the game was applied by Rev. Thomas Wilson, a Puritan minister of Maidstone, England who wrote in 1700 that he deplored the playing of "baseball on the Lord's Day." (Odd! So did William A. Hulbert, founder of the National League!)

The term "base–ball" was used in the *Little Pretty Pocketbook*, published in London, England in 1744.

Naturally, the game followed English civilization to the New World where it was modified and called a variety of names. George Ewing, a soldier in the Continental Army, wrote home that he and his fellow revolutionaries passed the time at Valley Forge by playing the game of "base" in 1778.

Princeton University was the site of a game of "baste ball" in 1786, possibly making it the first college in baseball history, an honor equal if not superior than Princeton having taken part in the so–called first intercollegiate game of football in 1869.*

A book published in France in 1810 called a similar game "poisoned ball" which was played on a diamond–shaped field as opposed to the square field of other versions.

In the *Boy's Own Book*, published in London in 1829, yet another variation was called "Feeder" and was played in the "West of England and the metropolis." In "Feeder", the bases were laid out in the shape of a diamond.

Book of Sports, published in Boston, Massachusetts in 1834, repeated the rules of "Rounders" that appeared in *Boy's Own Book* five years earlier but with some minor variations, calling the game "Base, or Goal Ball".

Boy's Book of Sports, published in New Haven, Connecticut in 1839, contained the rules of "Base Ball" that had one important difference from any previous set of rules to any similar game. Prior to this, the bases were to be run in a clockwise direction. The Connecticut book ruled the bases were to be laid out in the shape of a diamond and were to be run counterclockwise.

Rounders (or baseball, stool ball, etc.) evolved into cricket in England but failed to develop beyond its basic rules in other countries.

During the first decades of the history of the United States, athletic clubs were formed by well–to–do gentle–

* **Some authorities on sports history, including this one, argue that the Princeton–Rutgers match of 1869 was actually the first inter–collegiate game of soccer to be played in this country and that the first real football game wasn't played until a few years later when Harvard met Yale in a game in 1875 after playing McGill University from Canada the year before.**

men as a symbol of their social standing; to be accepted from membership was a badge of elitism. Ostensibly, these organizations had the purpose of providing their members with a place for recreation, entertainment, and exercise. A gent could engage in a physical activity, such as jogging or calisthenics, if he was so inclined; or he could wile away the hours smoking, drinking, and gambling — not with cards and dice but by betting on the club's source of income: its prize fighter. The membership would hire a fighter, pay him a salary, arrange his bouts, back their man with bets, then divvy up the winnings — provided he won, of course. This system wasn't applied to other sports such as billiards, swimming, pigeon shooting (real live pigeons, not the clay ones used by latter–day skeet shooters), quoiting (pitching a kind of round horse shoe at a stake in the ground), pedestrianism (high speed walking), rounders, and baseball because the members played these activities themselves.

The first known association to regularly play any game *resembling* baseball was established in Camden, New Jersey during the spring of 1831, but if it had a name, it wasn't reported to the local newspaper. Later that year, a second group in Camden formed the Olympic Ball Club for the purpose of playing "town ball" on the 4th of July as part of the holiday festivities. These two groups met in the first match between two different organizations later that summer, then merged into the Town Ball Club of Philadelphia in 1833.

Other games were being played in the United States that resembled baseball, but these weren't really baseball because of their square–shaped playing fields and the rule that bases were to be run clockwise.

Alexander J. Cartwright drafted a set of rules for the playing of baseball by the Knickerbockers, a gentlemen's club established on September 23, 1845 for the purpose of exercising together because they worked at sedentary professions. Cartwright's rules called for four bases only and presupposed that they should be laid out in a diamond shape.*

The first recorded instance of a game played under Cartwright's rules by two organized aggregations, as opposed to a pick–up game between a bunch of guys with nothing better to do on a Saturday afternoon, occured June 19, 1846 between the Knickerbockers and the New York Base Ball Club on the Elysian Fields in Hoboken, New Jersey. Cartwright was the umpire, and the New York Club won, 21–1, because 21 was set as the winning score, the same as in ping–pong. The next recorded game between two clubs wasn't played until June 3, 1851 when the Knickerbockers downed the Washington Club of New York.

The Knickerbockers were the first club to adopt a uniform when in 1849 they determined their playing costume would consist of blue woolen pantaloons, white flannel shirt, and chip (straw) hats.

The Washington Club merged with the Gotham Base Ball Club in 1852. No games were played between clubs that year, but the new Gotham Club met the Knickerbockers twice in 1853. A third club, the Eagle Club, was formed in the spring of 1854, and the Empire Club and the Excelsior Base Ball Club were established that fall. The Putnam, Eckford, and Atlantic clubs of Brooklyn

* Actually, the field was supposed to be diamond–shaped but wound up being a square like the modern infield. The term diamond stuck because the square was set on one corner, giving it the appearance of a diamond instead of a square.

and the Union Base Ball Club of Morrisania, New York joined the field in 1855, and dozens more came into being the year after.

On December 4, 1856 at a meeting of the Knicker-bockers, a resolution was passed calling for "a general Base Ball Convention" of "the various Base Ball Clubs of" New York "and vicinity" with "each to select three representatives to meet at 462 Broome Street, in the City of New York, on Thursday, the 22nd day of January next, at half-past seven o'clock P.M."

At this 1857 meeting, the first set of codified rules was drawn up for games between the competing clubs. A total of 16 clubs were represented at a gathering in May, and one important rule change was made. No longer would 21 runs scored by one side constitute a match; henceforth, a match would be nine innings. The matter of tie games wasn't taken up at this time.

A second "Convention" was held on March 10, 1858 at 298 Bowery, the Gotham Club's headquarters in New York; and 26 clubs with two delegates each were repres-ented. At this conference, "The National Association of Ball Players" came into existence. It was hardly national in substance with all but one of the clubs being located in Manhattan or on Long Island; the New Brunswick, New Jersey club the lone exception. A year later 49 clubs were represented at the third annual meeting. During this time period, Cartwright's rules were called the "New York game" because they were almost exclusively played by clubs located in and about New York City. In Massachusetts and Pennsylvania, versions of rounders were still being played by most clubs. The Tri-Mountain Club of Boston was the first to be formed in that city that played baseball, beginning play in 1858. The first baseball game wasn't played in Pennsylvania until 1860.

On July 20, 1858, the first game between nines representing two different cities was played by all–star teams from Brooklyn and New York City. An admission of 50 cents was charged, and nearly 4,000 fans were in attendance, including several dozen professional gamblers who were giving odds to all comers. This was the first recorded instance of money being involved with baseball, and money meant professionalism wouldn't be far behind.

James Creighton was a pitcher for the Niagara Club in 1858, and he was one of the best around. The following season he was "tempted" to play for the Stars of Brooklyn and moved to that club with George F. Flanley. In 1860, the Excelsior Club offered Creighton several "inducements" to play for them. Creighton and Flanley accepted compensation in spite of Rule 36 of the National Association's by–laws that specifically forbade any player receiving monetary considerations or the equivalent for playing the game.

This same Excelsior Club became the first organization to send its team on a playing tour. Beginning in Albany, the Excelsior nine spent two weeks in July 1860 traveling through upstate New York, playing games against the best local clubs and beating them all soundly.

With the establishment of the Eagle Club in San Francisco in late 1859, baseball under "New York rules" became the national game. At the annual convention in March 1860, 62 clubs were represented, including delegates from Boston, Washington, Detroit, Baltimore, and New Haven, Connecticut.

Baseball was pretty much the *private property* of well–to–do gentlemen until the Civil War when soldiers from all classes and walks of life were thrown together in military camps around the nation. The major forms of group recreation for these men were football and baseball. With the close of hostilities, veterans returned to their home towns, and suddenly, baseball was no longer the exclusive game of upper–crust gentlemen's athletic clubs. It belonged to the people and was being played by young men in almost every community in the land.

In the latter half of the 1860s, burgs of all sizes were fielding nines, and many of these were sponsored by leading citizens for one very specific reason: money. A successful baseball team was a source of civic pride; and a proud community was a prosperous, expanding city, meaning more people moving into the town and more dollars finding their way into the pockets of land speculators, bankers, landlords, storekeepers, tradesmen, mechanics, etc. Not only would a winning baseball team help to keep money moving in the same manner as any other good business, but it could also cause some instant good fortune for a small town because baseball wasn't just played for the thrill of competition. Rival teams played for high stakes. Occasionally, the prize was the take at the gate, but more often, it was a sizeable bet.

The custom of the time was for the two teams to make a wager, say $100. Each team would place the agreed amount in the hands of the umpire or some other respected neutral official. When the contest was played out, the winning team collected the money and divided it among the players and the organization sponsoring the team. Because they only received money for winning and not simply playing, ballplayers were still considered to be amateurs.

In reality, when large amounts were at stake, one or both teams *hired* a player or three — usually a pitcher — secretly paying them to play in that particular game.

These "ringers" were the first pros. In time, having a paid player on your team was acceptable, such as in 1864 when the Athletic Club of Philadelphia hired Alfred Reach to captain their team. It then became only a matter of time before a whole team went completely professional.

The convention of 1866 reiterated the National Association's stand of opposing professionalism, but the regulation wasn't enforced. In fact, the Atlantics of Brooklyn, the Mutuals of New York, and the Athletics of Philadelphia totally ignored the rule, as all three clubs compensated their players in one manner or another.

In the spring of 1869, baseball "devotees" — as fans were called in those days — were following the exploits of seven "professional" teams: the Mutuals of New York, Atlantics of Brooklyn, Athletics of Philadelphia, Cincinnati Red Stockings of Cincinnati, Nationals of Washington, Unions of Lansingburgh (Troy, N.Y.), and Excelsiors of Chicago. At least they were considered to be pros in 1869 by contemporary sportswriters. Some latter-day historians don't consider all of them to have been pro nines. These revisionists make a distinction between professional and semi-professional that differs greatly from the meanings of the two terms in 1869.*

* During the 1870s, Henry Chadwick, one of the first great journalists in America whose specific job was to write and edit sports copy, determined that a professional team was one where each player was paid a salary; a semi-pro team was one where some of the players received a salary and some didn't; and an amateur team was one where none of the players openly took a nickel for playing. Chadwick also identified the "co-operative team" which was one where the players

Of the above listed clubs — and that was what they were, athletic and baseball *clubs* with memberships that could number in the hundreds — the Cincinnati Base Ball Club of Cincinnati, Ohio was the first club to openly hire a full team and pay all of its players salaries, making it — according to the revisionists — the first professional team in the history of baseball. The Mutual Club of New York, the Atlantic Club of Brooklyn, and the Athletic Club of Philadelphia had been paying salaries and gate receipts to *all* of their players — who were also club members — for a few years prior to the Cincinnati Club's move. The argument still rages that one of these three teams was actually the first pro nine in history. For that matter, the same Cincinnati Club was paying salaries to its captain, Harry Wright, and four other players in 1868 and was compensating the remainder of the squad in other ways.

Born in England and raised on cricket playing, Harry Wright was hired by Aaron B. Champion, president of the Cincinnati Club, to captain and manage the Red Stockings — nicknamed so for the garish crimson socks the players wore — in 1868. Wright then brought in four more players to play with the best of the local talent. When the Cincinnati boys proved to be inadequate against the eastern teams, Wright hired additional players for the 1869 season. The Cincinnati roster listed Asa Brainard, P (pitcher); Doug Allison, C (catcher); Charlie Gould, 1B (firstbaseman); Charlie Sweasy, 2B

received some sort of financial consideration, such as a portion of the bet or a percentage of the gate receipts. But above all, Chadwick declared any man who accepted money for his baseball services to be a professional player.

(secondbaseman); Fred Waterman, 3B (thirdbaseman); Wright's brother George, SS (shortstop); Andy Leonard, LF (leftfielder); Wright, CF (centerfielder); Cal McVey, RF (rightfielder); and Dick Hurley, substitute. Each one of these men received a salary for playing baseball.

The Red Stockings traveled over 11,000 miles in 1869, winning all but one game — and that was a tie — out a total of 57 played. They finally tasted defeat at the hands of the Brooklyn Atlantics on June 14, 1870 but not before sparking the imaginations of baseball enthusiasts all across the country and exciting them with the spectacle of the professional game. More losses, rising expenses, and increased player salaries brought on the demise of the Cincinnati Club later that year of 1870, but the initial financial success of the Red Stockings, both at the gate and at the betting window, forced existing pro teams to follow Cincinnati's example, if for no other reason than to keep pace with the Queen City of the Ohio River. It also encouraged magnates around the country to found more professional teams.

2

"The Failure of Base Ball Here"

Baseball in Chicago was best summed up at the beginning of the 1869 season by the New York *Tribune*:

> Perhaps the only thing in which Chicago has not put forth efforts to outstrip New York is in a ball club. A professional organization exists there, which is the city's pride, but its playing strength has not been sufficient to make even a respectable stand against the heavy clubs outside. The Excelsiors may be doing something to bring up the club to first–class playing merit; but, if so, they are doing their work very quietly.

Indeed, too quietly as it turned out.

The Excelsior Base Ball Club of Chicago (not to be confused with the club of the same name in New York) was a financial failure during the 1868 season because the team was a loser on the field and the competition for entertainment dollars was high. Other Chicago nines faced the same problem. The only solution was to disband or merge. But the baseball situation wasn't always that bad in Chicago.

Baseball clubs began springing up west of the Alleghenies in the late 1850s, beginning with the Franklin Club of Detroit in 1857. The Civil War inhibited the growth of the organizations sponsoring teams but didn't stop it completely. Every town of any size had at least one club; e.g., Rockford, Illinois, a small city of approximately 7,500 people had three clubs in 1865. The metropolis of the West, Chicago, had more than a dozen at that time, and these spawned several dozen more over the next few years. Baseball was so popular that whenever nine men of similar ilk, such as carpenters, muleskinners, stock brokers, etc, came together in one place they made up a team and challenged other teams to play them. These were not athletic clubs; they were mostly tradesmen's groups out to have some fun and pick up a little loose change by playing the game.

The athletic clubs, such as the Atlantics, Athletics, Garden Citys, etc., took the game much more seriously. They played for sporting honor and bigger purses. Chief among these was the Excelsior Base Ball Club, headed up by G. Charles Smith.

On December 6, 1865, representatives of 15 western clubs met at the Briggs House in Chicago and formed the North–Western Association of Base Ball Players. At the forefront of this new organization stood the Excelsior Club. The Excelsiors had been the best in Chicago in 1865, defeating all comers. A year later they were considered to be the top nine in the entire Northwest, beating all challengers in the Great Lakes region.

The only team to seriously contend with the Chicagoans was the Forest City Club of Rockford that was led by a 16–year–old pitcher named Albert Goodwill Spalding. Playing with Spalding on that team were the

already famous Bob Addy and the soon to be famous
Ross Barnes.

Chicago's baseball devotees were extremely proud of
their Excelsiors, and the local newspapers boasted
mightily about the prowess of their team. With thumbs
in suspenders, patrons of the Excelsiors would extol the
virtues of this player or that and state unequivocally that
his equal wasn't to be found on any eastern nine. No nine
could beat the Excelsiors, the best team in the West,
making them the best team in the country — bar none!

Then the summer of 1867 rolled around, and the
National Club of Washington, D.C., embarked on a
western tour, the first such trip ever undertaken by an
eastern nine. The Nationals featured a young shortstop
named George Wright who the year before had
"jumped" from the Gotham Club of New York to the
Union Club of Morrisania in July. Although only 20
years old, Wright was made captain of the Washington
nine and was listed as a "government clerk" by the club
which otherwise included "federal employees and college students", all ostensibly *amateurs*. In reality, the
entire team was professional; the only reason the players
were on the government payroll was to play baseball for
the National Club.

When the Nationals departed Washington, their party
included the National Association's president, Arthur P.
Gordon; baseball writer Henry Chadwick; and about 10
"gentlemen having enough interest in players and the
game to accompany the Nationals on their tour." The
Nationals pounded western clubs in Columbus and Cincinnati, Ohio; Louisville, Kentucky; Indianapolis, Indiana; and St. Louis, Missouri before finally arriving in
Chicago for a tournament that included Rockford's
Forest City nine with Al Spalding, the Chicago Atlantics,

and the Excelsiors.

Earlier in the month the Excelsiors had beaten Spalding and his teammates by the narrow scores of 45–41 and 28–25. The locals figured the Washington nine would suffer the same fate after Rockford bested the Nationals, 29–23, in the opening game of the tournament. Little money had been bet on the outcome of the Rockford–Washington game, but the Chicago gambling fraternity came to the fore the next day when the Excelsiors were to play the visiting club from the nation's capital. An enormous crowd turned out to see the contest; admission was 50 cents a head; but they all went home disappointed as the Nationals mauled the locals, 49–4. The bettors traveling with the Washington party cleaned up, and the Chicago *Tribune* cried that the loss to Rockford was a put up job for the purpose of securing bets. Joe Medill, the newspaper's publisher and majority owner, printed a reluctant retraction after a visit to the newspaper by some officers of the National Club and their attorneys who threatened severe legal action if the publisher didn't "admit" to making a mistake.

For some odd reason, Chicagoans of the 1860s and early 1870s couldn't bear defeat. To them, a team that couldn't win every game was tantamount to having a team that couldn't win any games. This attitude was fostered by the Chicago press, which seemed to think like Chicken Little when he was struck in the noggin with an acorn: one loss and the sky was falling.

Immediately after the defeat by Washington, local journalists, who had been crowing about the enormous prowess of the Excelsiors only the day before, did a 180-degree turn and viciously attacked the Excelsiors as being totally worthless.

This marked the beginning of the end for the Excelsiors. With their egos severely bruised, they became prey for many local clubs, and unable to face the humiliation of being on a loser, most of the better players drifted to other towns to play.

Unable to muster a decent nine themselves for the 1869 season, the Excelsior Club joined with the Eureka Club to form an outfit known as the Amateur Base Ball Club, which was what the players were because not one of them was paid a salary or a portion of the gate receipts. The Amateurs were considered to be the best of the bunch in the Garden City, but they still couldn't measure up to the Forest City Club of little Rockford. This was too much for many Chicagoans to bear. Something had to be done.

Throughout 1869, Lewis Meacham of the Chicago *Tribune* gave all sports good coverage, but baseball was particularly well mentioned. Almost everyday the newspaper ran its *Sporting Matters* column. One day it would have stories on horse racing, swimming, baseball, and quoiting. The next day it would be pugilism, pedestrianism, baseball, and swimming. The day after the feature would have reports on pigeon shooting, pugilism, baseball, and horse racing. Although it would give lots of ink to the other sports, the tabloid devoted most of its coverage to baseball games played by several area teams, while also reporting on the more famous nines from other locales, especially the exploits of the Cincinnati Red Stockings. Hardly a day passed that summer that the *Tribune* didn't mention Chicago's Aetnas, Amateurs, and Actives; Evanston's Gazelles; Rockford's Forest Citys; Cleveland's Forest Citys; New York's Mutuals; Philadelphia's Athletics; Brooklyn's Eckfords and Atlantics; or the Haymakers of Troy, New York.

There were also stories about games played between in-
dustrial teams within the city or contests played by nines
from different cities but who were in the same line of
regular work, such as the boards of trade from Chicago
and Milwaukee. There was even a game played between
the printers and reporters from the city's various newspapers.

But throughout all these stories, something was missing. It was an intangible called emotion. The items
printed about baseball resembled the cold, hard facts of
an almanac. They were dull and uninspiring. For the
most part, their words were unimaginative and repeti-
tive. In short, they were a bore.

With the merger of the Excelsior and Eureka clubs at
the beginning of the season, Meacham heaved an editorial sigh and wrote that the resulting Amateurs were
better than nothing. He was wrong.

Not all of the best players from the Excelsiors and
Eurekas remained in Chicago to play that summer.
Many of them fled to other cities where they could get
paid for playing or were at least given good paying jobs
with time off for baseball practice and games. Those that
stayed in the Garden City were hard pressed to make up
a competitive nine. In fact, the only teams they could
beat were other Chicago nines, and few of these could
even compete with clubs from other cities in Illinois. It
was a most embarrassing circumstance for the largest
city west of the Alleghenies to be without a quality baseball team.

So as summer waned, one baseball man in the Chicago
area couldn't stand the embarrassment another day and
started the wheels rolling toward putting a real professional team on the field that would be, at the very least,
competitive with the other professional clubs across the

country. But because several efforts to form a first class organization in the past had failed, this valiant leader acted in almost total anonymity, *announcing* his intentions in the August 28, 1869 issue of the *Tribune* thusly:

> *To the Editor of the Chicago Tribune*:
>
> Will you please inform me who the parties are appointed to receive subscriptions for the proposed "Invincible Base Ball Club of Chicago." It will certainly be a favor duly appreciated, as myself and many others are both anxious to send in some stamps, and know what has already been done toward putting in the field a "nine" intended to meet and entertain the Athletics, Haymakers, Red Stockings or any other men of the "bat" that may come to our city on a professional visit.
>
> Yours etc.
>
> John Smith.

John Smith? Now really!

His real identity was Thomas J. Foley, a professional billiards player who hailed from Cashel, Ireland, having been born across the Atlantic on August 16, 1842. Although no one knew it at the time, Tom Foley was about to change baseball history in Chicago. Another article appeared in the *Tribune* four days later on September 1, 1869 under the heading, *The Failure of Base Ball Here:*

> Base Ball in Chicago
>
> We take great pleasure in publishing the following letter from an esteemed correspondent:

To the Editor of the Chicago Tribune:

It seemed to me very strange, while reading in the Detroit *Free Press*, nearly a month ago, that so large an amount as $20,000 had, in one day, been subscribed for the purpose of bringing together a "nine" that might excel, at least, our country cousins at Rockford.

Base ball is a game quite as interesting in our city as at Cincinnati or New York, if properly contested, and we are fully as anxious to have an "invincible" club as any other city in The Union. Why it is I cannot say, but Chicago is certainly among the poorest at the bat.

Muscle appears to be wanting, and, judging from the kind of game some of our amateurs play, one would be led to suppose that more practice, or a change of men, would produce better pitching, better catching, and no doubt better fielding. The Garden City boys have no relish for these facts, I presume; no one blames them, nor have others a desire to have them brought to light, who feel a pride in Chicago enterprise.

"John Smith" says he would like to know something about the proposed "invincible base ball club of Chicago." The information would indeed be acceptable to all of us. If $20,000 is not enough to put the ball in motion, pass around again the subscription paper and you shall have more.

P.D.

P.D. hit the right note when he wrote: "It seemed to

me to be very strange . . . ."

Strange indeed! No such subscription had ever been put forth, meaning $20,000 hadn't been raised toward the formation of a professional baseball club in Chicago. The *John Smith* letter was a plant written by Foley *and* Meacham for the sole purpose of stirring up interest in such a project as the establishment of a legitimate pro nine. *P.D.*'s letter had all the appearance of being a part of the scheme begun by *Smith*. Meacham continued the charade by commenting in length immediately after *P.D.*'s letter:

> Our correspondent but echoes the ideas of thousands in this community. There is no doubt of the fact that, as a base ball centre, Chicago is a failure. It is humiliating enough to make that acknowledgement, but still it is bare truth. We gain nothing by concluding otherwise. It is true we have other achievements to fall back upon as a community. That such even our worst enemies and most bitter rivals will concede. But that only makes the fact more glaringly patent, that there is one thing Chicago cannot succeed in, and this — base ball. There was a time when Chicago thought otherwise. Our people went to work organizing a base ball club, with the same energy that they would build a tunnel or construct a railroad. This was some years ago. We then thought we had a base ball club that we could bet on. We did bet on it! That club was the lamented Excelsior. They grew as suddenly into notoriety as a mushroom into existence. They beat everything around

Chicago — candymakers clubs, the dry goods clerks clubs, the newsboys clubs, and the bootblacks clubs. And then they grew ambitious. Chicago grew ambitious with them. The Excelsiors became venturous; Chicago became venturous also. And then the celebrated Nationals, of Washington, were played with. It is unnecessary to recur to that event. It is not only unnecessary, but humiliating. Not only is it humiliating, but painful suggestions and memories of certain losses, occasioned by a too great confidence in local base–ball prowess, will arise at such recurrence. Suffice it to say that the Excelsiors were beaten; not only beaten but that it was only through a great stretch of courtesy that the Nationals allowed them to make a couple of scores. This defeat was not only a damper to the rising hopes of Chicago, but it was a deathblow to the club. It has never been heard of since. It has ceased to be of the present, and has passed into history. All there is left of it is a certain inquiring couplet inscribed over the doors of the club room:

"If so early I was done for,
Wonder what I was begun for!"

Since then there have been numerous attempts made to organize other base ball clubs. But they wouldn't stay organized. The Excelsiors were not phoenixes, and wouldn't arise from their ashes. We have now probably a dozen organizations. They present numerous bats, divers balls, and sundry uniforms. Some of the members of these organizations spend the "midnight oil," and grow to look like students in getting the rules of the game by heart. There is no doubt that they have gotten these perfectly. There is no doubt that they understand the game, — understand it sci-entifically, too, — but they cannot play it! We regret to say it, but it is true. This is the Rubicon that cannot be passed. Every now and then these clubs will give an exhibition. They go out in all sorts of weather. They go with the necessary preliminaries of breaking and disjointing their fingers, spraining their ankles, callousing and enlarging their hands. They flatter themselves that now they can play! They send out their glaring announce-ments. A fine game of base ball by local clubs is promised, and crowds of local enthusiasts go out to observe and exuberate. The clubs are gotten up without too much expense. Their uniforms are showy, and their general appearance everything that could be desired. A generous public hales them with enthusi-asm. They come up to the scratch beautifully, and go to the club or field scientifically. But here the matter ends. They cannot do any-thing more, and least of all *play base ball!*

Now, what is the reason of all this? Why should the ambition of our citizens be thus balked? Cincinnati and St. Louis, and even Milwaukee clubs, play base ball. Why cannot Chicago clubs? We have the legs to run, the arms to bat and throw, the hands to catch; we have the eyes to see "flies," the judgment to calculate distances, and citizens with feet big enough to cover bases. But, with all this, we cannot play base ball.

Is it in the climate? Or the stars? Or in ourselves? Is it because of the lake? No; for Cleveland and Milwaukee have good clubs. Why, then is it? Is it from some mysterious cause like that which gives our girls big feet and "cheeks of sorry grain," and causes our policemen to be such immense swearers?

Everybody here plays at the game. Every park, public square and enclosure has some who are practicing with the ball. Every employer who has a sufficient number of hands to form a nine is called upon to give a day to his men, who have challenged the hands of some other employer to a match game of base ball. We have all the disagreeable concomitants of the fever, without any of its beneficial results. But it seems to be of no use. All of our efforts appear to be vain. There is some insuperable bar to our proficiency which we cannot remove. We might as well give it up first as last. It will cost us both tears and pangs, but it will save us both money and mortification to drop the matter altogether. It is of no use. What a people cannot do they cannot. This is plain common sense, and we certainly have got that. As a city we only should do those things which we do well, and which reflect credit on the grand old town. At base ball we simply make ourselves ludicrous. The only class of our citizens who are successful with clubs are our policemen. Our base ballists are not. Let us accept the situations gracefully.

Bury My Heart at Wrigley Field

In the following days, more letters to the editor and more snide remarks by Meacham appeared in the *Tribune*. Each correspondent helped piece together the reasons behind the sad state of the pro game in Chicago, and two overriding factors became evident: Professional baseball was seemingly opposed by the press and by a large number of local businessmen. Both factions looked upon the sport as belonging to amateurs and boys; playing it for profit was "in bad taste." The sentiment shown by the correspondents reflects above all that baseball players were considered to be lazy, drunken bums who made poor employees. If a man belonged to a baseball club and it became public knowledge, he was likely to be dismissed from his job. Because of this attitude of the business community in general — and not as a whole — the best players in the Garden City left Chicago and sought situations in other cities where they could earn a living and play baseball, too.

As Meacham stated in the *Tribune*, baseball — at least on the professional level — was a failure in Chicago in 1869. But not for long.

3

Chicago Goes Pro

A wag once said: "Nothing is ever accomplished by a committee unless it consists of three members, one of whom happens to be sick and another absent."

Fortunately for baseball fans in Chicago, the committee that wanted a professional team in the Garden City consisted of only two men, and both of them were determined to see that the job was done right.

Who were these two men?

One was Tom Foley, the champion billiards player and well known gambler who also owned an establishment that was a combination saloon, billiards parlor, and pool hall. In 19th century jargon, a pool hall was a gambling den, not a place to play billiards; a pool was a wager. Foley was well respected by the finer folks of Chicago. Among his acquaintances were Marshall Field, Potter Palmer, Joseph Medill, and George Pullman. He was also friends with the shadier element of the city but kept that part of his life quiet so as not to soil the other.

The other man was Lewis Meacham, the only sportswriter in Chicago at the time. Meacham was a regular news reporter for the *Tribune*, but he loved baseball. He was the first newspaper man in the city to give running accounts of the important games and the first to print box scores. His work with the *Tribune* forced the other

Chicago dailies into covering baseball. Alfred H. Spink wrote in his 1910 history of baseball that "Meacham, like all the first lot of baseball writers, wrote of the game only out of pure love for it and without any thought of profit or future reward."

Foley and Meacham knew each other well as it was the latter's duty to cover the billiards matches of the former for the *Tribune*. Together, they conspired to bring professional baseball to Chicago. Meacham worked on the public openly through the pages of the *Tribune*, while Foley buttonholed the wealthiest men of the community at every opportunity at his business and at the various social clubs of which he was a member in good standing. Gradually, they wore down the opposition until the time for creating a new baseball club was ripe.

On Friday October 1, 1869, a meeting was held in the gentlemen's parlor of the Briggs Hotel in downtown Chicago and was attended by approximately 50 interested businessmen and social leaders. With their cigars in one hand and their brandy snifters in the other, these gentlemen called on S.W. Tanner to chair the conference, then elected Fred Erbe to the post of secretary. W.H. Anderson then stood and assured the gathering that the Chicago Board of Trade (CBT), of which several of those present were members, would support any endeavor to produce a professional nine for the city and would make generous contributions to that end. Anderson's pledge carried an enormous amount of weight, putting everyone there on notice that the CBT felt a professional team would be a financial benefit to the city. Erbe put forth a plan to forego creating the usual stock association and instead utilize an organization that would resemble a limited partnership. Erbe's plan was taken under consideration, and George

Treadway, Matthew Renner, W.H. Anderson, F.H. Tanner, and F.W. Budd were appointed to a committee to determine the best method of raising funds for a team and to find a suitable permanent playing field. The meeting was adjourned until the following Thursday.

The next week on October 7, 1869 acting President S.W. Tanner appointed W.H. Anderson, W.F. White, and a Mr. Lowe to a committee to write a constitution and by-laws for the new club. Tanner then appointed T.Z. Cowles, F.W. Budd, J.W. Bute, Mr. Overrocker, and Mr. Gray to a committee to study how to set up a permanent organization. George Treadway reported that there was a great deal of interest in a professional team being shown among the businessmen in Chicago. This reflected a switch from earlier attitudes toward the game and its players. Previously, many employers deplored baseball players, calling them loafers on the job when they bothered to show up for work at all. But no talk like this went on that night, and an adjournment was called until the following Tuesday.

That auspicious evening finally arrived on October 12, 1869. President Tanner called the meeting to order at the Briggs Hotel, and immediately requested the reports of the committees he had appointed the previous week. Meacham reported the event in the *Tribune*:

> The Committee on Constitution and By-Laws reported in effect that the organization shall be known as the "Chicago Base Ball Club." Members shall be elected by ballot, and five negative votes shall constitute a rejection. The usual provisions are made as to honorary membership, payment of dues, etc. The officers of the club

consist of a President, such a number of Vice Presidents as the club may from time to time elect; a Treasurer, a Recording Secretary, a Financial and Corresponding Secretary, and an Executive Committee, consisting of five members, said committee to appoint a Business Manager, and to attend to the miscellaneous affairs of the club in general. The report was adopted.

The committee on nominations reported the following officers to the club:

President — Potter Palmer.

Vice Presidents — W.F. Wentworth, General P.H. Sheridan, J.M. Richards, W.F. Coolbaugh, H.C. Wentworth, C.B. Farwell, F.E. Morse, S.J. Medill, F.B. Wilkie, I.N. Higgins, J.C. McMullen, W.C. Cleland, J.W. Midgely, Robert Harris, A.M. Smith, Geo. M. Pullman, W. Sprague.

Treasurer — D.A. Gage.

Recording Secretary — J.W. Bute.

Correspondence Secretary — T.Z. Cowles.

Executive Committee — S.W. Tanner, W.S. Walker, Fred Erbe, Matthew Renner, F.S. Fauntleroy.

The report of the committee was adopted, and the officers named therein declared elected.*

This was an incredible array of shakers and movers within the community. Potter Palmer was the founder of the company that became Marshall Field & Company, and he was the builder and owner of the most luxurious hotel in Chicago in the 1870s. Gen. Philip H. Sheridan

* John C. Galt was not listed in this article but was among those elected as vice-presidents.

was one of Grant's top lieutenants during the Civil War and was then in command of all western military forces. J.M. Richards was president of the Chicago Board of Trade. W.F. Coolbaugh owned the Union National Bank. Charles B. Farwell was a millionaire dry goods merchant. W. Frank Wentworth, H.C. Wentworth, J.W. Midgely, John C. Galt, W.C. Cleland, Robert Harris, and A.M. Smith were all railroad executives: McMullen, chairman of the board with the Alton & St. Louis R.R.; Cleland, president of the Fort Wayne & Chicago R.R.; Harris, chairman of the Burlington and Quincy R.R.; and Smith, chairman of the Rock Island and Peoria R.R. S. Joseph Medill was one of five men who had purchased the *Tribune* in 1855 and as its publisher turned it into one of the leading newspapers in Chicago. F.B. Wilkie was the publisher of the Chicago *Times*, and I.N. Higgins was the publisher of the Chicago *Republican*. George M. Pullman was the founder and owner of the Pullman Palace Car Company. T.Z. Cowles was the brother of Alfred Cowles who was one of Medill's partners in the *Tribune*. D.A. Gage and his brother George founded Gage Brothers & Co., a leading wholesaler of millinery located at Madison and Wabash in the Loop.

Meacham made little to do about the group of gentlemen who organized the Chicago Base Ball Club, but that was an intentional oversight. Characteristically of newspaper publishers of those days, Joseph Medill was playing it safe by declining to take any credit for having part in the founding of the new club — just in case it failed. Instead, he had Meacham play down the role of the *Tribune* men.

Although several prominent men were listed as officers of the new club, they were officers in name only, especially the long list of vice-presidents. To be a member of the most prestigious baseball club in Chicago was a real feather in a gentleman's social top hat. Put up a little money, and get a title. But to be an active officer and do the work? How utterly revolting! Use the name, use the money, but use the man? Not likely!

No, the real work fell to the members of the executive committee, but even these men weren't very effective. They talked a great deal, but when it came right down to someone getting the job done, the responsibility was foisted onto the shoulders of one person, and he wasn't even an officer of the club — yet. The committee appointed Tom Foley to be manager* of the Chicago Base Ball Club.

But why Tom Foley? It must be remembered that in 1869 gambling — at least the corrupt New York variety — had yet to stick its ugly head into baseball and a professional billiards player was socially and morally acceptable because he was a sportsman and only gentlemen were sportsmen. Besides, Foley was a winner. He was the best there was in Chicago with a cuestick, and to be associated with him was as desirable then as it would be in later years to be associated with any great athlete. He was also a charmer, having quite a reputation with the ladies, which did nothing to slight his standing with contemporaries who considered sexual prowess to be the manliest of attributes.

So the executive committee turned to Foley immediately that night, charging him with the responsibility —

---

* Manager is a misleading title in modern terminology in that he didn't *manage* the team on the field but performed the duties of a modern front office general manager, business manager, ticket manager, and traveling secretary.

although exacting a promise of secrecy from him at the same time — of forming a new nine for Chicago. Foley took one look at the club treasury and accepted the challenge of becoming the manager of the infant organization.

In less than two months, Foley and Meacham brought to fruition their dream. Step by careful step, they had planned their work and worked their plan:

> August 28 — the bogus letter from *John Smith*;
> September 1 — the letter from *P.D.* of Detroit;
> September 1 — Meacham's scathing commentary on *The Failure of Base Ball Here*;
> October 1 — the first meeting at the Briggs House;
> October 7 — the meeting of the executive committee;
> October 12 — the constitutional meeting establishing the organization.

Foley had cajoled his rich friends into forming a new club, and Meacham had persuaded his readership to accept it as Chicago's very own. By the end of the evening of October 12, 1869, the Chicago Base Ball Club — and thus the Chicago Cubs — was born.

4

Jimmy Wood
and the First Cubs

It's often said that whatever happens in Washington takes two years or more to be felt across the country. This adage was proven true in 1869 with the formation of the Cincinnati Red Stockings and the Chicago Base Ball Club.

The Washington Nationals were a team made up of government clerks and college students from the nation's capital. In 1867, they toured the country, playing all comers and usually blowing them off the field. One of their victims was the best team in Ohio, the Cincinnati Base Ball Club. The Nationals totally destroyed the pride of the Cincinnati club by defeating its team so badly that the stockholders gave the boot to the organization's officers and reinstated former president Aaron B. Champion to lead them back to glory.

Champion wasted no time as he raised enough money to spend $11,000 refurbishing the team's playing field. He then brought in Harry Wright to manage and captain the club's team and entrusted Wright with $15,000 more with which to hire ballplayers for a professional nine. Wright signed up four pros in 1868 to play with an equal number of amateurs, but this team still couldn't match

up with the better nines from New York and Philadelphia. So he hired four more play-for-pay boys for the
1869 season, and the all-professional Cincinnati Red
Stockings were thus born.

It was this same Washington team that also helped to
bring about the founding of the Chicago Base Ball Club.
Actually, when the Nationals brought on the demise of
the Excelsior club, the establishment of the new organization became necessary. With the founding of the
Chicago Base Ball Club on October 12, 1869, optimism
began peeking through the cold midwestern winter that
Chicago would once again have a professional team that
it could be proud of. The club's manager, Tom Foley,
was openly touring the East, playing billiards matches
wherever he went, but secretly he was meeting with
several different baseball men.

Rumors about this player and that player were softly
whispered in sporting circles throughout the city as
Foley kept his fellow club members informed about his
activities with frequent letters and telegrams, but
nothing definite appeared in print until late in the year
when the New York *Sun* reported that the Chicago Base
Ball Club had signed Jimmy Wood, a secondbaseman
who had played for the Brooklyn Eckfords the summer
before; he was to be paid $2,000 a year. Lewis Meacham
denied this rumor at the time by writing a strong editorial
against it in the *Tribune*, but it proved to be true.

Jimmy Wood was the first player that Tom Foley
signed to a contract with the new Chicago Base Ball
Club, and thus, he was the first Chicago Cub.* Wood was

* The signing of Wood, as with most ball players in those
days, was done secretly because one club didn't want
the other clubs to know what they were doing. Because

also given the position of team captain, which made him the first field manager in Chicago Cubs' history.

On January 16, the day after the first meeting of the club's stockholders in 1870, a *Tribune* editorial complained that nothing was being done toward acquiring a first-class team and what was being done was being bungled by inept persons who weren't named in the article. The writer even went so far as to conclude that the club was a failure and insinuated that the organizers were fraudulent hucksters who had bilked the subscribers out of their money. The writer's biggest gripe was the fact that most of the best players in the country had already been signed by other teams. Because of this, he called for the immediate cessation of activity and the disbanding of the club before any more money was wasted on a nine that wouldn't have the very best players on it.

From the style and content of the editorial, the author of this column could only have been Joseph Medill, the newspaper's publisher and a prominent stockholder in the Chicago Base Ball Club. Medill was already notorious for being a skinflint, and only he would dare to complain so openly about how the club was being operated. Fortunately for Chicago's baseball fans, this whining inkslinger wasn't heeded.

Meacham countered Medill's venom by publishing a letter from a *reader* who signed himself as "Justice" and who took the trouble to explain that baseball was a team game with nine integral parts that had to mesh properly

of this practice and the fact that all the papers of the Chicago Club were destroyed in *The Great Chicago Fire*, no definite dates can be given to Wood's contract or those of the other players signed by Foley.

in order to be efficient. *Justice* pointed out that the Cincinnati Red Stockings had gone undefeated in 1869 with players who weren't considered to be the best in the land as individuals at their positions but who worked together so well that no other nine could best them. The opinionated missive rejected Medill's complaints that a very competitive team hadn't been secured, reminding him that the top men at each position were scattered among the teams of the East, leaving Chicago with many of the second best players in the country. *Justice* completed his argument by stating that the men so far hired would make up a solid aggregation and do Chicago proud.

The largest contributors to the new club had been unable to attend the Saturday night gathering about which Medill had gotten so wrought up, so another conference was hastily called for the next Monday January 17 at the Briggs House. At this meeting, elections were held and new officers installed. They were D.A. Gage, President; W. Frank Wentworth, Vice–President; W.F. Tucker, Treasurer; W. Lowe, Recording Secretary; J.W. Bute, Corresponding Secretary; and J.H. McVicker, Philip Wadsworth, Gilbert Dutcher, Albert Crosby, and Thomas Foley as the Board of Trustees. Tom Foley was finally being given some of the power he needed to run the club.

In spite of Medill's protestations and complaints, things were being done toward securing the best players available for the new Chicago nine. With Jimmy Wood already under contract, Foley and his new captain went about signing up men to fill the other three infield positions and the three outfield spots. The temporary roster read:

Michael James "Bub" McAtee 1B
James Wood 2B
Marshall Ney "Mart" King 3B
Charlie Hodes .... SS
William "Clipper" Flynn .... OF
Edgar E. "Ned" Cuthbert .... OF
Fred Treacy .... OF

With the seven field positions already in place, the only thing remaining to do was to hire a battery and a substitute or two. A month later the New York *Tribune* listed the new Chicago nine among the country's growing number of professional teams, although stating the Garden City squad couldn't yet be taken seriously as one of the better contestants for the mythical crown of the coming season because it had yet to prove itself as a cohesive unit on the playing field. The Cincinnati Red Stockings were at the top of the New York writer's list, followed by the Mutual Club of New York, Atlantic Club of Brooklyn, Athletic Club of Philadelphia, Chicago Club of Chicago, Union Club of Morrisania, Eckford Club of Williamsburg (Brooklyn), and Haymaker Club of Troy. The Tri–Mountain Club of Boston, Olympic and National Clubs of Washington, and Maryland Club of Baltimore were also mentioned as being more or less pro teams.

Another month passed before the first team roster was finally filled up by Foley and Wood with the signings of pitcher William Charles "Cherokee" Fisher, catcher James Laurie "Deacon" White, and Levi Meyerle, a thirdbaseman and change pitcher.*

* A change pitcher relieved the regular starter when he tired during a game or needed a day's rest.

Meacham aroused interest in the players by giving brief biographical sketches of them in the *Tribune*.

At age 26, Jimmy Wood had already spent more than a third of his life playing organized baseball. He had formerly played with the Eckfords of Brooklyn, and he worked as a machinist during the off–season.

Cherokee Fisher pitched for the Haymakers of Lansingburgh (Troy) in 1869. He was only 24 but was considered to be one of the oldest hurlers in the country. Fisher started his pro career with the West Philadelphia Club in 1866. At the end of the 1867 campaign, he joined the Diamond State Club of Wilmington, Delaware. In 1868, he was with the Buckeye Club of Cincinnati. He was a butcher by trade.

Bub McAtee, 24, also left the Haymakers for Chicago. He was a painter when he wasn't playing baseball.

Charlie Hodes was one of the youngest of the new Chicago nine at 21, but he had already played two seasons at shortstop for the Eckfords before moving west. A near six–footer he had the lithe form of a great defensive infielder. During the off–season, he earned his living as a printer.

Mart King was another deserter of the Haymakers. Henry Chadwick, the first great baseball writer and pro- moter of the game, called King the best centerfielder in America at the turn of the decade. King was a farm boy who joined the Troy nine right after the Civil War and was a seasoned veteran at "the ripe old age of 22" when he signed on with Chicago.

Deacon White, 23, was the only player without a national reputation to join the Chicago nine in 1870. Primarily an infielder with the Forest City Club of Cleveland in 1869, he was slated to catch for Chicago.

Clipper Flynn was the youngest starter on the new

team at 20. A brushmaker in the off–season he played nearly every position with the Haymakers during the three years he was in Troy, but Jimmy Wood planned to have him in right field for Chicago.

Ned Cuthbert was also a butcher when he wasn't "a knight of the willow" as baseball players of that day were often poetically called. He started his pro career in Philadelphia playing for the Keystones for three years, 1864–66. In 1867, he switched to West Philadelphia Club for half the season and the Athletics for the other half. He remained with the Athletic Club throughout 1868 and 1869.

Fred Treacy was the only player who had a previous Chicago connection before signing on with the new Chicago club in 1870. He had started his career in 1867 with the Franklins and Excelsiors of Brooklyn, then joined the Excelsior Club of Chicago the following year. In 1869, he was back in Flatbush, playing for the Eckfords.

Levi Meyerle was the youngest member of the team at 19, but he wasn't short on experience. Like so many other baseball players of his day, he began his career before finishing high school. At the age of 16, he was pitching for the Harry Clay Club of Philadelphia. The next year he joined the Geary Club and had Doug Allison, the Red Stockings' catcher, behind the plate for his pitches. In 1869, the Athletics of Philadelphia signed him as a full–time substitute.

Toward the end of March, Foley and Wood agreed to let a certain fellow named Tremaine try out for the team as a pitcher. Tremaine hailed from Smith's Creek, Michigan and claimed to have played two years with the Niagaras of Buffalo and the previous season with the Beavers of Newcastle, Canada, supposedly the best team in the Dominion. Because spring was barely upon the country, regular playing fields weren't ready for action, so Foley arranged to hold the audition at Washington Park on North Clark Street in spite of the signs telling everyone to stay off the grass. Wood brought out the whole team as well as a few local players, and a game was to be commenced. The players were just beginning to warm up when three policemen came along. Flynn and McAtee saw "the blue–coated minions of the law" first and immediately made their departure without warning the others. They ran as fast as they could to Foley's saloon about a mile away and breathlessly reported that the others had been arrested for trespassing on public property.

Foley was beside himself until Wood and the boys came traipsing in a few minutes later, equally out of breath, having made their escape as well.

And Tremaine? Another practice was arranged for the following day at Lake Park, but the youngster from Michigan failed to impress Wood and didn't make the team.

Tremaine's tryout on March 23, 1870 was the unofficial beginning of spring practice for the Chicago Base Ball Club's team. Besides the occasional outdoor exercise when the weather permitted, the players were given the use of Kormendy's Gymnasium where they "were allowed to visit daily, taking exercise in leaping, lifting, club swinging, etc."*

With the eastern papers raving about the quality team that the Chicago club had signed, the *Tribune* began singing a different tune about the fortunes of

---

* The "clubs" mentioned in the article weren't baseball bats but Indian pins, which were used for toning muscles as opposed to building them with weights.

baseball in the Garden City. Meacham covered for his boss by stating that all the negativism of the winter was meant to spur on the management of the Chicago Base Ball Club. The truth of the matter was Medill didn't know all that much about baseball and felt he was expressing the opinion of the majority. Meacham wrote that the popularity of baseball was sweeping the country — Chicago included — and that the prospect of having a professional nine of any sort excited even the fair weather fans in the Garden City.

Only one minor problem disrupted the new team's pre–season practices. Before signing a contract with Chicago, Deacon White had signed on with the Forest City Club of Cleveland for the 1870 campaign. Thinking he could secure a release from the Ohio organization, he inked the agreement with Foley. Instead, the Forest City officials demanded he fulfill his bargain made in Cleveland. Foley tried to persuade the Ohioans to let White come to Chicago, but they were adamant about their position. White returned to Cleveland.

To replace White, Foley signed Bill Craver, a catcher who had been with the Troy Haymakers in 1869. Besides Craver, Foley also signed lefthanded pitcher Ed Pinkham who had been "the man in front of the bat" for the Eckfords of Brooklyn the year before. The addition of Pinkham was necessitated by the desertion of Fisher, who "revolved" to the Haymakers, i.e., he reneged on his deal with Chicago and went back to his old team.

There were no rules in 1870 to prevent "revolving" by players.

During this time, the National Association of Base Ball Players was still an operating entity but a powerless one in all respects except one: the NABBP made the playing rules.

From the earliest days, "base ball" rules favored the batter unfairly. Admittedly, the pitcher stood only 45 feet from the plate, but he was forced to *pitch* the ball to the batter, i.e., propel it forward underhanded. And this had to be done without bending the arm at the shoulder, elbow, or wrist. Whipping the ball toward the plate as latter–day softball pitchers do was strictly forbidden.

Throwing motion wasn't the only disadvantage faced by the hurler. The rules simply stated that the batter could inform the umpire where he wanted pitches de-livered to him, shrinking his strike zone to as much as one–foot square over the heart of the plate. In other words, the pitcher had to serve up a fat pitch every time or the pitch was called a ball or a "wide". This made the strikeout a real rarity. Fortunately, walks weren't as numerous as one would think — the base–on–balls was much more infrequent than the big K because not to hit a ball was considered unsportsman–like — because it took three, four, five, or more "wides" in a row to get one ball called and nine balls to get a walk.

In 1870, the strike zone was defined as being any-where over the plate between the top of the batter's head and a foot above the ground. No longer could the striker call for his pitch to be in an exact spot, but he could still call for high or low pitches. Instead of calling a ball or a strike on every pitch that wasn't swung at, the umpire had to determine whether the pitcher was missing the plate on purpose or by accident or whether the batter was deliberately letting a good pitch go by. If the ump felt that the pitcher was trying to *fool* the hitter into swinging at a bad pitch or that he was trying to delay the game, the ump had to warn the pitcher that another "wide" without a good pitch for the hitter to swing at would result in a ball being called. However, if he felt that the batter was purposely letting good pitches go by in order to delay the game or rattle the pitcher, the official had to warn the hitter that another pitch in the strike zone without a "wide" first would be called a strike if he didn't swing at it. And if this wasn't bad enough, it still took nine balls to get a walk.

Three other important rule changes were made in 1870. No longer could a team walk off the field in the middle of the game due to a disagreement with the umpire and be declared the winner. To leave the field was to forfeit the game. If a game was in the bottom half of an inning with the *last–to–bat* team ahead and it started to rain, then that team could be declared the winner. No longer was it necessary for both teams to finish an inning in order for a game to be considered complete.

The final change made the host team responsible for the crowd. The new rule determined that a ball was dead after being touched by a spectator until it was returned to the pitcher in the pitching box, and until this time, no runners could advance. This prevented the home crowd from interfering with play to the advantage of their team.

As April unfurled and the weather improved, the Chicago nine played various practice games with local amateur clubs and "picked nines".* The Aetnas provided the opposition most often, but they were no match for the pro team. On April 9, with Pinkham pitching, Chicago rocked the amateur squad, 35–15, in a six–inning affair.

The next day the *Tribune* reprinted an article from the

* The first nine bodies who wanted to play ball that day.

New York *Times* that listed all the pro clubs in the
country, their locations, and the method of paying their
players. The sportswriters in Chicago didn't second–
guess the New York writer as to which team was professional and which wasn't. They simply accepted the
listing as fact.

CLUBS	LOCATION	SYSTEM
Atlantic	Brooklyn, N.Y.	Share gate money
Athletic	Philadelphia, Pa.	Pay by salary
Cincinnati	Cincinnati, Ohio.	Pay by salary
Chicago	Chicago, Ill.	Pay by salary
Eckford	Brooklyn, N.Y.	Share gate money
Forest City	Rockford, Ill.	Share gate money
Irvington	Irvington, N.Y.	Share gate money
Keystone	Philadelphia, Pa.	Share gate money
Kentucky	Louisville, Ky.	Pay by salary
Mutual	New York.	Pay by salary
Maryland	Baltimore, Md.	Pay by salary
National	Washington, D.C.	Appointed to office
Olympic	Washington, D.C.	Appointed to office
Olympic	Baltimore, Md.	Share gate money
Olympic	Philadelphia, Pa.	Share gate money
Tri–Mountain	Boston, Mass.	Pay by salary
Union	Lansingburgh, N.Y.	Share gate money
Union	Morrisania, N.Y.	Share gate money

By modern standards, this list contained only seven
real professional clubs. By 1869 standards, the two
Washington teams were included because the players
were given government jobs as compensation for playing
on the club nine; they were pros by reality but amateurs
by technicality. Using Henry Chadwick's yardstick of
the early 1870s, the nine "share gate money" teams were

co–operative clubs and the two Washington clubs were amateurs.

At long last, the day for the first *match* game of the season turned up on the calendar. Foley and Meacham accompanied the team as they traveled south on their first ever road trip. The date was April 29, 1870, and the place was St. Louis, Missouri, which, considering how the Cubs and Cardinals have been rivals for so many decades, was only appropriate. To mark the occasion, the Chicagoans donned their new uniforms, and their first nickname was pinned on them by Meacham. As he reported it in the *Tribune*:

> . . . It consists of a blue cap adorned with a white star in the centre, white flannel shirt, trimmed with blue and bearing the letter C upon the breast worked in blue. Pants of bright blue flannel, with white cord, and sup– ported by a belt of blue and white; stockings of pure white British thread, shoes of white goat–skin, with the customary spikes, the en– semble constituting by far the showiest and handsomest uniform ever stated by a base ball club. Already the snowy purity of the hose has suggested the name of "White Stockings" for the nine, and it is likely to become as generally accepted, not to say as famous, as that of the sanguinary extremities.

For the next two decades, the Chicago baseball team would be commonly known as the White Stockings, the Whites, the White Legs, or the White Socs, White Socks, or White Sox, depending on which newspaper one read. The Union Club of St. Louis was no match for the

White Stockings as Chicago took the measure of the Missouri nine, 47–1. Fred Treacy was the hitting star for the Whites, scoring five runs and pounding out seven hits. He also made a fine running catch of a fly ball. Pinkham was the winning pitcher, going the distance — a not too uncommon feat in those days.

After soundly defeating another St. Louis club, the Whites continued their first–ever road trip to New Orleans. In turn they defeated the Atlantics, 51–0; the Lone Stars, 18–10; the Robert E. Lees, 24–14; and the Southerns, 41–9. Unlike many northern cities, New Orleans permitted baseball games on Sundays and for good reason. Chicago played the Lone Star Club on Sunday, May 8, 1870, and drew a crowd of 3,000 spectators. The combined attendance of the other three games, each played on a week day, was less than 1,500. If not for the Sunday game, the trip to the Crescent City would have been a pecuniary failure for the Chicago club.

From Louisiana, the White Stockings worked their way north, their first stop in Memphis. Meacham wrote about how well the players were being treated off the field while they were in St. Louis and New Orleans, and Memphis gave them no less a welcome:

> . . . and proceeded direct to the Overton House where a suite of elegant rooms were allotted to them.

Then he noted the physical condition of the players but did so in a manner that was almost humorous:

> Not one of the party was feeling well, the change of water since leaving home having

begun to show its effect in producing bowel complaint.

Fortunately, they were rejuvenated with large medicinal doses of brandy and Jamaica ginger in time to play ball that afternoon. Too bad for the Bluff Citys because the Chicagoans gave them the same treatment that Crazy Horse and the Sioux gave Custer at the Little Bighorn: Chicago 157, Memphis 1.

The last stop on the tour was in Kankakee, Illinois, where the Grove City Club offered to play the White Stockings. They shouldn't have been so nice: Chicago 111, Kankakee 5.

Upon returning to Chicago, Medill boasted mightily about the Chicago Base Ball Club. This was the same man who had berated the efforts to form a professional organization the previous winter. Now he was bragging how great the White Stockings were and how the Chicago nine was better than the Red Stockings of Cincinnati. This was an awfully large claim because the Chicagoans hadn't beaten another *pro* team yet. All eight opponents on their trip had been amateur or semi–pro teams — by 1869 standards — made up of strictly local talent.

In spite of the 8–0 record and the semi–vacation in the South, not all was peaches and cream with the White Stockings:

> There is yet, however, vast room for improvement in the personal feelings and relations of the various members, the general tendency being toward petty backbiting and jangling. This can only be overcome by time and a firmer controlling power than has yet been

exercised. Time will do its share, and Jimmy
Wood *must* do the rest. He has a difficult task
— more difficut than would ever be suspected
with the club at home — but we believe he is
equal to it, and that when the proper time
arrives he will surprise some of the trouble–
some, turbulent elements of his team with a
check both sudden and effectual.

After knocking off two Chicago amateur teams, the
Amateurs and the Garden Citys, at Ogden Park, the
Whites took a train to Janesville, Wisconsin to play the
Badger State champs, the Mutuals; defeated them,
74–5; then went to Milwaukee to take on the Cream Citys
and whipped them, 71–19. It was rapidly becoming more
and more apparent that there was a wide gap between a
pro team like the Chicago White Stockings and any
strictly local amateur nine. But a true test of the Chicago
Club's quality was on the horizon.

Although the Forest City Club of Cleveland wasn't
among the professional clubs listed in the New York
Times, the Ohio nine was a pro organization. The Cleve–
land club might not have been a national nine like the
White Stockings, but it was pro all the same with players
recruited from all over Ohio.

The Cleveland team scheduled a match with the
Whites to be played in Cleveland later in the year when
the Chicago nine headed east on a tour, but before that
day arrived, the Forest Citys went on a tour of Indiana
and Illinois. While they were in Chicago to play some of
the local amateur nines during the first week of June
1870, the temptation to play the new professional squad
from the Garden City proved to be too much for the
Cleveland management. A game between the White

Stockings and Forest Citys was arranged for June 3, 1870.

The White Stockings weren't supposed to play Cleveland when they did because Tom Foley had promised the Rockford club that they would be the first pro opponent for the Whites. As a pretense toward keeping his word, the contest with Cleveland was called the contest a *practice* game. Neither team took it that way as they played with their regular lineups. Approximately 4,000 fans turned out to watch Chicago win, 15–9, but not without being tested to the limit by the Cleveland nine.

The White Stockings played two more amateur teams, the Garden City Club of Chicago and the Actives of Clinton, Iowa, defeating them, 24–11 and 96–7 respectively, before they played host to the Forest City nine of Rockford.

The Rockford game was the one affair that every fan in the upper Midwest had been waiting for; this was the true test for the new professional club. Rockford was considered to be the best in the West because they had Al Spalding pitching for them. He was the only pitcher to beat the Washington Nationals during that club's western tour a few years earlier, and many thought Spalding to be the best hurler in the land. This stop in Chicago was the last for the Rockford club on their 18–game tour. So far, they had won 13, lost but 3, and tied one. They had met and beaten some of the best teams in the country, including the Brooklyn Atlantics and the Washington Nationals. Spalding had been everything everything short of brilliant, and now the Forest Citys were ready to take on the upstart Chicago club.

An unprecedented throng of over 12,000 crowded into the stands and overflowed onto the playing field of Dexter Park, the horse racing track located five miles southwest of downtown Chicago, for the first *official* pro home game of the Chicago White Stockings, June 16, 1870. Rockford won the coin toss, so the White Stockings came up to bat first. Spalding wasn't ready to pitch yet, but the umpire called for the game to begin. The Chicagoans took advantage of Spalding's tight condition and rattled him for 15 runs in the first inning and seven in the second. By the time he settled down in the third, the White Stockings were up, 22–0. Rockford tried to get back into the game with a rally in the fourth, but Pinkham relieved Meyerle to put out the fire. The Whites coasted home with a 28–14 win, and all of Chicago was delirious with baseball fever. The Garden City had a winner!

The White Stockings were the best in the West and the South at least, but they still hadn't faced any of the eastern teams — the other pros. This was soon to be remedied with a trip to the East that was to start with the Cleveland Forest Citys. Chicago's record to date was 17–0 overall and 2–0 over professional teams with wins over Rockford and Cleveland at home.

By the time the Whites reached New York City, their marks were extended to 27–0 overall and 5–0 over pro nines, as they added victories over Cleveland, the Troy Haymakers (the White Stockings' first extra inning game, June 27, 1870), and the Boston Tri–Mountains. But all good things seem to come to an end sooner or later. The Brooklyn Atlantics, the same team that handed the Cincinnati Red Stockings their first–ever defeat a few weeks earlier, handed the White Stockings from Chicago their first loss, 30–20, on July 5, 1870. A second loss followed when the Whites faced the powerful New York Mutuals. This minor losing streak was halted the next day when the White Stockings defeated the

Morrisania Unions, 28–12.

At Philadelphia a day later, Meacham, who was once again traveling with the team, screamed about how the umpire completely favored the Athletics, especially in the late innings when the home team had several batters reach first on walks. The White Stockings lost their third game of the eastern tour. The Chicago club finished the road trip with more games in New York, Philadelphia, Washington, and Baltimore, winning seven in a row, four of the wins coming over pro teams. Upon returning home in July, the White Stockings' record had climbed to 35–3 overall with a pro mark of 10–3. The trip proved costly to the players. Several of them were ill or banged up with minor injuries. Mart King contracted a fever and remained in his home town of Troy in order to recuperate under the care of his family's physician and his mother. Pinkham was too injured to play, so Foley hired a fellow named Burns of the Rose Hill Club of St. John's College in New York as a replacement pitcher. Wood, Hodes, and Craver were playing hurt.

The first opponent for the White Stockings on their second home stand of the season was the Mutual Club of New York. Wood sent Burns to the mound, and the new hurler did a fairly good job of stopping the Mutuals, but the Chicago hitters failed to solve the servings of the New York pitcher as the Mutes gave the Whites their first home loss and first ever shutout in their short history, 9–0, Saturday, July 23, 1870. The New York *Herald* chortled that henceforth it would not longer use the terms "skunked, whitewashed, or goose–egged" when a team was held scoreless. From that time forward, the newspaper's word would be "Chicagoed" which would only be appropriate considering some of the meanings of English translations of Chicago, such as "stinking water" and the like.

The Chicago press reacted to the defeat in much the same way that they had when the Union Army suffered its first defeat at the hands of the Confederates in the First Battle of Bull Run. Someone had to pay for the disaster, and frankly, the reporters didn't care who got the axe as long as some blood was spilled.

When the Harvard College Club dumped Burns and the battered White Stockings, 11–6, the editorial screams grew more shrill and nervewracking. The only paper that gave the Whites the benefit of the doubt was the *Tribune* probably because that sheet had a reporter traveling with the team at all times while the others only covered the Whites when they played in the Chicago area.

However, it didn't last. When the White Stockings were beaten again, this time by the Philadelphia Athletics, 19–11, Medill joined the chorus of detractors and called for Jimmy Wood to resign as captain of the team and for other changes in the lineup. The publisher almost got his wish.

At the next monthly meeting of the Chicago Base Ball Club's stockholders, the Chicago *Journal* reported, as quoted by the New York *Tribune* in an article reprinted by the Chicago *Tribune* , that Norman T. Gassette was elected president and the management of the organization was handed over to an executive committee made up of the president, vice–president, treasurer, and secretaries. This replaced the board of trustees that had dictated policy to Tom Foley, often tying his hands at crucial moments.

There were some changes on the field as well. After losing three straight, Burns was moved to right field, and Meyerle was once again the regular pitcher. George

Keerl of the Garden City Club was hired to fill in at shortstop as Hodes was moved to first base. The move worked as the White Stockings trampled the visiting New Orleans Lone Stars, 42–8.

Confident that they were back on the winning track, the Whites welcomed the Troy Haymakers to Chicago. It had taken Chicago 10 innings to down the Haymakers, 25–21, in New York. That was when they were all healthy. In Chicago, with half the team still hurting, Troy took the measure of the White Stockings, 16–11. The victory wasn't that sweet, however.

Prior to the season, Foley had signed Cherokee Fisher to pitch for Chicago and advanced the hurler $200 toward his salary. When Fisher "revolved" to Troy, the Haymakers' management said it would repay the money if Chicago would release Fisher from the contract. Foley agreed, but Troy didn't send the money, only a promise to pay the Chicago Base Ball Club when the Whites came to New York for a game. Even then the Troy manager refused to pay the $200. Foley let the Haymakers' boss off the hook — for the time being. Finally, when Troy visited Chicago for the return game, Foley held back the amount owed from Troy's share of the gate receipts. As far as the Chicago Base Ball Club was concerned, the Fisher affair was now closed.

The White Stockings got back on the winning track again with victories over the Baltimore Marylands and the Washington Olympics. Chicago used three players from local amateur clubs in these games. After wins over the Aetnas and Athletics of Chicago, the club management expelled Bill Craver from the team for gambling and general disobedience of most of the club's rules. Craver "published a card" in the *Tribune*, claiming he was being made an example, that he hadn't done anything that the other players hadn't done, that his only "crime" was refusing to play sick. Time proved Craver was the liar.

Firing Craver didn't do much to improve the team's play. The Whites dropped their next game to the Rockford Forest Citys in spite of hiring a new infielder, an Irishman named Ed Duffy, that Foley lured away from the Brooklyn Eckfords because Duffy was tired of not having steady pay. The addition of the veteran Duffy did help the Chicagoans to avenge themselves on the Brooklyn Atlantics, 12–4, when the latter nine visited the Garden City in late August.

Finally, the day for the big game of the season arrived. The White Stockings were in Cincinnati to take on the Red Stockings, and Medill, back home in Chicago, fully expected the Chicago nine to get beaten. But something strange happened to the Whites that September afternoon. They played their best game of the year, defeating the mighty Reds, 10–6, behind Pinkham.

The people of Chicago reacted as if the White Stockings had just been declared the greatest team of the year. Fully 3,000 citizens turned out to greet the players on their arrival back in Chicago. "Nevan & Dean's band" led a procession of carriages from Union Station to the Briggs House. Perched on the front seat of the lead carriage was a month old pig wearing red stockings on its feet and a placard around its neck that read: "Porkopolis, Sept. 7, 1870." Cincinnatians didn't take too kindly to having their city and the defeat symbolized this way, but they would have done something similar had they been in the same position as the Chicagoans.

After defeating the reigning national champions, the White Stockings embarked on one last eastern road trip with the purpose of proving to everyone that their victory over Red Stockings was no fluke and that they were the best in the land.

The tour started in Cleveland where the Forest Citys played gracious hosts off the field but gave the Chicagoans everything they could handle on the diamond before losing a close one, 9–7. Pinkham picked up his 15th win of the season overall and fifth against pro teams.

Then it was on to New York to play the two Brooklyn teams and the Mutuals, especially the Mutes because they had been claiming the title since the White Stockings had bested Cincinnati and they had defeated Chicago, not once, but twice. Jimmy Wood and the players figured they needed to beat the New Yorkers soundly in order to lay any claim to the mythical championship.

Pinkham rose to the occasion against the Eckfords and Atlantics, holding each team to single-digit totals. The batsmen did their parts for Chicago, outscoring the Eckfords, 22–8, and the Atlantics, 9–4. Then it was showdown time with the Mutes.

The White Stockings built an early lead, adding to it as the game progressed. Pinkham baffled the New York hitters with his lefthanded deliveries until the last three innings of the contest, but by that time, Chicago was leading by an insurmountable margin. The Mutuals' late rally against Meyerle fell very short as the Whites downed New York, 22–11, and put forth their own claim to national honors.

At this point, the Whites had amassed an excellent 47–8 overall record and a 19–7 mark against the so-called professional teams. These won–loss numbers were as good as any team's marks in the country, but won–loss records weren't the supreme method of determining a champion. Who you beat, how often you beat them, and who beat who last counted more. Because of this imperfect system, Foley wanted one more game with the Mutuals and one with Cincinnati to make the White Stockings the undisputed champs.

The New York teams had promised to visit Chicago once more before the snow began to fly, and the Red Stockings were due to play one game in the Garden City before the season officially ended on Thanksgiving Day. Harry Wright and the Cincinnati management kept its bargain with Foley, but the Mutuals stayed home, refusing to play any more games that "counted", stating in an early October news release that all games played by them henceforth would be considered practice games and would have no bearing on the national title which they claimed as their own.

From baseball centers all over the nation, club members, players, fans, and journalists raised an incredible cry of indignation. Even the New York *Tribune*, which considered the White Stockings with their 20–7 pro record to be champs because they had soundly whipped the Mutes in their last meeting, belittled the Mutuals for taking such a childish stand by refusing to surrender the "whip–flag"* to Chicago.

Undaunted, the Chicago Base Ball Club's leaders had their own pennant made as soon as the White Stockings nipped the Cincinnati nine again, 16–13, and proudly displayed it in Tom Foley's saloon. Foley tried to give the Red Stockings one more shot at the Chicagoans, but the weather and finances interfered, denying the Ohio

---

* The whip–flag, the symbol of baseball supremacy, was a large pennant that the winning club was entitled to fly over its field for the next season.

team its last opportunity to repeat as national champs.

The White Stockings were accepted as being the best in the country by nearly every baseball expert except Henry Chadwick who naturally stood by the Mutuals because he had a vested interested in the New York club. The Whites had the better record for the season, and they had beaten all the same clubs that the New Yorkers had. Although some historians in later years also sided with Chadwick — mostly because they accept him as being the *only* baseball authority of his time when actually he was only one of several highly opinionated writers of that era and because he was from New York — the newspaper records of the day plainly indicated the championship belonged to the Chicago Base Ball Club's White Stockings.

The people of Chicago were so excited about their professional team that the newspapers were already printing stories about the 1871 team in November 1870. The White Stockings were accepted as being the best in the country for 1870, but Medill and many Chicago fans felt there was room for improvement. After all, the White Stockings had lost those eight games in 1870.

5

When Mrs. O'Leary's Cow Became A Goat

It simply wasn't true that Mrs. O'Leary's cow was responsible for beginning the saddest tradition in all of
sports history. Wasn't it bad enough that the poor beast
was blamed for *The Great Chicago Fire*? After all, the
Cubs (nee White Stockings) proved over the decades
that they could blow pennant races all on their own.
They didn't need any help from a bovine in 1871 any
more than they needed any help from a goat during the
years between World War II and the Dallas Green era.

When the 1870 baseball season ended, the world
famous Cincinnati Red Stockings had passed into glory,
Harry Wright was on his way to Boston, and the Chicago
White Stockings were considered by most to be the new
champions of the United States.

The ascendency of the Chicago Base Ball Club to the
pinnacle of baseball's mountain was acknowledged at
the fall convention of the National Association of Base
Ball Players when a resolution was passed whereby the
Chicago team was duly recognized as having been the
best in the land for 1870. With that settled — over Henry
Chadwick's and the New York Mutuals' protestations —
the representatives of the various clubs got down to

business.

Tom Foley and Jimmy Wood represented the Chicago Base Ball Club at the annual confab in New York, held on the last day of November. When a resolution was made calling for the condemnation of professional baseball, they led the charge to vote it down, 17–9. But they failed to stop a proposal to play in 1871 with a less lively ball, to use a so-called "dead ball" instead.

This new rule was made specifically to thwart Chicago because of the hitting success achieved by the White Stockings in 1870. And everyone knew it. The new ball had to contain no more than one ounce of rubber and measure nine and a quarter inches in circumference. The ball of 1870 had been made with more rubber and was slightly smaller, making it livelier and hotter to handle when hit.

There were other rule changes as well. A batter was still permitted to step forward to strike at the ball, but he could no longer go past the front edge of the home base. In previous years, a pitcher could *intentionally* walk as many men in an inning as he liked, but for 1871, the rule was changed to put a halt to pitchers who abused the privilege of skipping lethal hitters in the opposing nine's lineup. Should a pitcher intentionally walk three men in one inning, it was grounds for a forfeit. But once again, it was left to the umpire to determine when the pitcher was intentionally walking a batter.

The strike zone was also changed for 1871. No longer would it be over the plate between the batter's head and a foot off the ground. In the coming campaign, the strike zone would be over the plate from the top of the batter's shoulder to his knee. A batter could still call for his pitch, but in 1871 he could only call for a high or low pitch, meaning above the waist or below the waist.

The final bit of business before the convention was the case of Bill Craver, the player that the White Stockings had dismissed in the middle of the season. Jimmy Wood was all for barring Craver from the NABBP for life. He found more than enough support among the delegates, and Craver was banned from playing for any club in the organization. It turned out to be a hollow punishment.

Throughout the winter, baseball rumors flew across the pages of the nation's newspapers. Some of them had quite a bit of truth to them; others didn't. Among the true ones was the fact Harry and George Wright had found backers for a new club in Boston and were planning to call the team the Red Stockings.

Things were changing in Chicago as well. Foley released Clipper Flynn, Charlie Hodes, and Levi Meyerle. Flynn and Meyerle had the urge to return to their respective home towns of Troy and Philadelphia, so Foley was doing them a favor. Hodes was a victim of numbers; the White Stockings had too many men under contract — or so Foley thought.

The winter roster included returnees Mart King, Bub McAtee, Jimmy Wood, Ed Pinkham, Ed Duffy, Ned Cuthbert, and Fred Treacy.

The newcomers were pitcher George "The Charmer" Zettlein from the Brooklyn Atlantics, outfielder Joe Simmons from Rockford, change pitcher and substitute Ed Atwater from Cincinnati, and substitute *Tom Foley from Rockford*. This Tom Foley, although bearing the same name, was no relation to the Chicago Base Ball Club's manager.

In January 1871, the annual stockholders meeting of the Chicago Base Ball Club was held, but only 12 members showed up. Norman Gassette was re-elected presi-

dent of the club, and Ed Thacher was re–elected sec–
retary. Thacher then pushed through an amendment to
the by–laws that reduced the number of officers to two —
the president and secretary — and put all the power to
run the organization in the very capable hands of
Gassette. This allowed Gassette to hire and fire as he
wished, and he wished to retain Tom Foley as the busi–
ness manager of the team and Jimmy Wood as its captain
and field manager.

The *Tribune* reported February 19 that Ned
Cuthbert's wife was experiencing "an elevation of the
spinal column about something or other." This was
fancy talk for her having her back up about Cuthbert
playing in Chicago again and leaving her behind in Phila–
delphia. She told her husband to play in Philadelphia or
get a divorce. Ned stayed home. Foley was furious, but he
let it go and resigned Charlie Hodes to replace him.

In 1870, the White Stockings had played their home
games at Dexter Park, the horse racing track located five
miles from the city's center, making it inconvenient for
folks to get there by foot. They either had to own a
carriage or take a day train out to the park as no streetcar
lines went out that far yet. This was a distinct drawback
for attracting large crowds. Another point against
Dexter Park was the location of the grandstand to the
playing field; spectators were seated too far from the
action to really get into the swing of the game. Therefore,
plans were made and ground was broken to erect a new
ball park between Randolph and Washington streets
along the lake front. Union Grounds would have a
covered two–tiered grandstand behind home plate and
down both sidelines as far as third and first bases. From
there to the outfield fence would be bleacher seats. The

whole park would be enclosed with a six–foot wooden fence painted white.

Also during the winter of 1870–71, Harry Wright corresponded with the executives of the other professional clubs throughout the country and expressed to them his thoughts on the need for an organization strictly for professional teams. He proposed they all meet in New York in March and discuss the matter. The other magnates concurred, and the first convention of professional ballplayers was set for March 17, 1871.

At this meeting, the National Association of *Professional* Base Ball Players was formed and a set of by–laws adopted. James N. Kern of the Philadelphia Athletics was elected president, then he appointed various persons to several committees to conduct the National Association's business.*

The first of these was the membership committee. It determined that any club that paid $10 to the NA would be eligible to compete for the whip–pennant of the organization. Nine clubs — the New York Mutuals, Boston Red Stockings, Philadelphia Athletics, Washington Olympics, Troy Haymakers, Cleveland Forest Citys, Ft. Wayne Kekiongas, Rockford Forest Citys, and Chicago White Stockings — chipped in a sawbuck each. The 10th pro team, the Brooklyn Eckfords, took a wait and see attitude.

Another group was the Judiciary Committee which

* Although the word *Professional* was the only difference in the name of it and its amateur counterpart, the pro group became known as the National Association from this day forward, and the older organization more or less faded into history.

had to administer the by–laws concerning "revolving" players. The NA passed a resolution that said no player could sign a contract with more than one team in the same year. If he did, then the Judiciary Committee would decide which contract was valid, whereas in the past the player made that decision.

Some players were notorious "revolvers". They would sign with one team, take some advance pay, then sign with another team that they really wanted to play for in the first place. The burned team usually had no recourse but to write off the lost money and try not to let it happen again. It was hoped that the NA would put a stop to this practice. Some argued it would; others opined to the contrary.

Right from its inception, the National Association was in trouble because it was a newfangled machine that was run with old–fashioned parts. The professional magnates were still thinking of their players as members of their clubs and their clubs as gentlemen's associations where good sportsmanship was practiced more than the Golden Rule. They still didn't understand that professional players were free agents who were for the most part without conscience, allegiance, or loyalty to any particular organization — including the fans who bought the tickets from which came the players' salaries. However, the players did display a remarkable affinity for the American greenback dollar by selling their services to the highest bidder.*

The owners also failed to recognize that baseball was

---

* The players would hold this same attitude repeatedly throughout the history of the game, particularly in the 1970s when free agency was restored, proving that history does repeat itself.

no longer a hobby or casual pastime for them but had become a serious business and needed to be treated as such in order to survive. Until both of these concepts were set into the thinking of the magnates, the National Association was a roaring lion without teeth or claws. Several players — at least those who were unscrupulous — figured this out this from the start and were ready to take advantage of the bumbling club executives.

Tom Foley instructed all the White Stockings' players to report to him in Chicago no later than March 15 because Jimmy Wood planned to take the team to New Orleans for spring training. All 11 players under contract checked in on time, and traveling manager Fred Erbe herded them onto the right train for the Crescent City. This was the first professional team ever to go south for pre-season *drills* and exhibition games.*

After a week of working out in the warm southern sunshine, the Whites played a series of games against the New Orleans teams and quickly learned that either southern pitching had gotten better or their own hitting had gotten worse over the year because the scores were much lower than the previous spring. Actually, it was the "dead ball" that had been legislated into the game to spite the White Stockings that was hurting Chicago's offense.

Before Jimmy Wood could come to this determination, he left the team to be with his ailing father in New York. He rejoined his teammates in St. Louis three

---

* The Whites Stockings and the New York Mutuals had gone south in previous years for exhibition games but never for the initial exercises of spring training as the 1871 Chicago team did.

weeks later in time to play in the nine's eighth straight exhibition win, but by then it was too late to do much to compensate for his team's lack of hitting because nearly all of the good hitting players were set to play for other teams and were therefore unavailable to be added to the roster.

The White Stockings opened their 1871 home season at their new park on the lake front with a pair of games each with Cleveland and Washington and single contests with Ft. Wayne and Rockford. Chicago won its opener, 14–12, over the Forest Citys on May 8, 1871, at the new park, Union Grounds, before a crowd estimated at 5,000. They swept all six pro matches as well as a pair of exhibitions before heading east on their first road trip of the campaign.

By the time they took the field against Harry Wright's Boston Red Stockings, the Whites were 19–0 overall and 6–0 in the NA. George Zettlein had trouble getting loose against the Beantown nine and trailed 14–5 after just four innings; but he finally settled down and his team-mates came through with some timely hitting as Chicago came back to win, 16–14, making Meacham delirious with superlatives in the pages of the *Tribune*.

Of course, most good things come to an end eventually, and the Whites' winning streak had its in New York a few days later at the hands of the Mutuals. Then to make matters worse and start Medill crying that the sky was falling, Chicago was dumped in turn by the Athletics and Olympics. The road trip wasn't as disasterous as he made it out to be. Jimmy Wood brought the team home sporting a 24–3 overall record and 7–3 mark in the NA, and prospects for another title in Chicago looked good.

Then things began going awry. Ed Pinkham and Bub McAtee started feuding with each other. The trouble

Bury My Heart at Wrigley Field

spread when Ed Duffy, the 27-year-old veteran of more than a dozen campaigns, took up Pinkham's side and Mart King sided with McAtee. The open argument threatened to divide the whole team as well as the fans, but before things got totally out of hand, Jimmy Wood restored peace.

Then the Chicago Board of Trade caused a problem when it began selling "pools" on the outcome of the NA's season. It wasn't bad enough that Tom Foley and the other professional gamblers were giving odds on the team already?

On June 25, the White Stockings were 8-3 in the pro circuit and in second place, a game behind New York. Five weeks later at the end of their second home stand, they were 12-4 and in first place in a virtual tie with Philadelphia at 13-5. By Labor Day, Chicago was still on top at 18-7, three wins ahead of the Athletics who were 15-7. The October 1 standings in the *Tribune* showed Chicago's record to be 21-9 in the pro loop and 46-15 overall. Philadelphia was 21-11, and Boston was 20-11. No other team was even close at this time.

The highlight of the summer was the game of July 28 when Boss Tweed's New York Mutuals came to town. Over 12,000 fans crammed themselves into the Union Grounds park to watch the White Stockings crush the Green Stockings from the Big Apple, 17-6.

That win vaulted the Whites into first place until the worst disaster of all struck Chicago.

For the most part, the summer of 1871 was terribly hot and dry across the United States; just about anything and everything made of wood was ready to be kindling at the first spark of a match. Farmers complained all over the nation that sparks from the railroad trains' wheels grating on the steel tracks were setting their fields afire. The national drought continued into autumn and was so bad that no rain at all fell anywhere east of the Rocky Mountains for the last two weeks of September and the first week of October.

The *Tribune* ran a regular column under the heading of **FIRES**, routinely publishing accounts of fires that occured elsewhere as well as in Chicago. Normally, the article ran only a few inches in length, only highlighting the more serious and fatal blazes.

But with each passing day of summer and fall, **FIRES** grew steadily in paragraphs and number of different stories as towns all across the Midwest reported an alarming increase in flaming disasters.

Things were so bad that many self-proclaimed prophets began preaching the end of the world was at hand and that all who failed to repent would soon be a part of the charred earth. These minions of the pulpit continued to spew forth their tirades of eternal damnation and hell-fire and were doing so on Sunday morning October 8 when the *Tribune* hit the streets reporting on more than three dozen major conflagrations currently and simultaneously raging in Michigan, Indiana, Minnesota, Wisconsin, New York, Ohio, Illinois, and several southern states. Whole forests and prairies were aflame. Cities and towns were losing whole blocks of buildings in but a few hours.

The Chicago paper particularly worried itself with a fire that had started the evening before in Chicago's West Division. The author of the story expressed grave concern over the strong wind that was blowing up to 25 miles per hour from the southwest, carrying sparks and glowing embers high into the night sky toward the few blocks between the main blaze and the Chicago River.

When the newspaper went to press that morning, the inferno had razed several blocks already and was still doing its evil best to destroy the city.

The rest of the world — those people outside of Chicago who received the *Tribune* and other Garden City newspapers by train either later in the day or the next morning — was left with a real life cliff–hanger because there were no papers printed on Monday and Tuesday in Chicago. Only rumors and unconfirmed reports of Nature's Armageddon were reaching beyond Chicago's city limits. Outsiders wouldn't find out for three days what happened to that first fire begun on Saturday night because a second blaze started up Sunday evening, originating in a barn on Chicago's southwest side. When the *Tribune* was able to go to press again on October 11, the public learned that the first fire which had begun on Saturday night had been contained and extinguished in the early daylight the next morning but that a second blaze had begun on the sabbath day and had destroyed everything south and east of the Chicago River as well as several blocks north of the river. It was the worst municipal catastrophe in the history of the United States in terms of property damage.

Every man, woman, and child in the Garden City was affected by *The Great Chicago Fire*, including the members and players of the Chicago Base Ball Club. When inventory was taken on the organization's second birthday just two days after the fire burned its last building, it was found that the club was bereft of everything short of its players. Gone to ashes were its ball park, clubhouse, accounting records, minutes of meetings, all its cash in a strongbox kept at the clubhouse, uniforms, and equipment; all lost to the rampaging inferno. Not only did the club suffer great losses, but so did most of its members and all of its players. Each one of the White Stockings lived in the burned out area, and each man lost nearly everything he owned except the clothes on his back. It was a horrible tragedy all around.

But life in Chicago went on. Immediately, the city began to rebuild, to resume its broad–shouldered way of life. Certainly, it was a disaster, but it wasn't the end of the world. It was a chance to begin anew, to create a planned metropolis instead of allowing haphazard growth with the march of time. The sun would rise again, and the White Stockings still had three home games to play and win for the National Association pennant.

Tom Foley knew it was senseless to attempt playing the games in Chicago. Even had they had a place to play and uniforms to play in and equipment to play with, who would come to watch them? Who felt like going to a baseball game when the city was in ashes? As loyal as Chicago fans were to their team — then as well as now — it was too much to ask of them. So Foley made arrangements to play these last contests on the road.

Wearing uniforms and using equipment borrowed from other clubs, the Whites lost all three games: two to the Troy Haymakers and one to the Athletics. The loss to Philadelphia allegedly gave the first National Association title to the Pennsylvanians.

Some historians blame *The Great Chicago Fire* for the White Stockings' late season demise and failure to cop the pennant. The Chicago nine was in first place when the city burned, and they did lose those last three games on the road. But the slump can also be attributed to the demoralizing effects of a newspaper article that appeared in the *Tribune* on September 22 in which the names of seven *new* ballplayers who would be playing

for Chicago in 1872 were announced. The factual ac‐
count gave more than half the team reason to be upset
with the club's management.

Those were good excuses for the late season collapse,
but they weren't the real reason the Chicago White
Stockings weren't crowned National Association
champs for 1871.

The truth of matter was the 1871 whip flag was legis‐
lated away from the White Stockings. At a special
meeting of the National Association held on November 3
in Philadelphia at which the White Stockings, the New
York Mutuals, and the Brooklyn Eckfords were not
represented, the Philadelphia Athletics were given the
first NA title.

The NA had a rule stating any player leaving one team
had to wait 60 days before he could play for another. The
Rockford club had used Scott Hastings in several early
games, all played within 60 days of his release by the New
Orleans Lone Stars, a team that was not in the NA.
George Hall was signed by the Washington Olympics on
May 9 after playing for a small town team in the East that
was also not a member of the NA.

At this special meeting in early November, a letter
from Chicago club secretary Ed Thacher requested that
games played by the White Stockings after the end of the
season on November 1 be counted toward the title to
replace the games that were cancelled by *The Great
Chicago Fire*. This request was summarily refused by the
Philadelphia men who were conducting the meeting.

The Philadelphia men then put forth a motion to have
all the games played by the Rockford Forest Citys before
June 16 forfeited because Rockford had played
Hastings. This motion carried. A similar motion to
forfeit the games of the Washington Olympics played

before July 9 because the Olympics had played Hall was voted down.

The final bit of business by this gathering was to discard all games played by the Eckfords on the grounds that Brooklyn didn't pay its $10 entry fee into the NA until after the Ft. Wayne Kekiongas had dropped out.

All this legislation affected the standings dramatically. When the NA was formed earlier in the year, the founders decided that the team that won the most games against the other NA teams would win the whip pennant. Attached to this rule was another that said the teams had to play a best–of–five series in order to have their games counted.

Prior to the special meeting in Philadelphia, the White Stockings had 21 wins, the Athletics had 21 wins, and Boston had 20 wins. These standings included games played with Rockford before June 16, with Washington before July 9, and with Brooklyn over the whole season. When the early games with Rockford were reversed and the games with Brooklyn discarded, the Athletics suddenly had 22 wins, Boston had 22 wins, and Chicago had 20.

The Philadelphia men had cleverly manipulated the meeting and had given themselves the title for 1871. Their legislation removed one win they had over Brooklyn but turned two losses to Rockford into wins. The White Stockings lost a win over Brooklyn and gained nothing from Rockford. Boston gained wins over Rockford but lost nothing to Brooklyn. By virtue of winning their season series over Boston, the Athletics were declared the NA champs.

If the games played by the Olympics before July 9 because of their use of Hall had also been reversed as they should have been, the White Stockings would have gained two wins, while neither the Athletics nor Boston would have gained anything. This would have created a virtual three–way tie for first, but the Whites would have to have been declared the NA winners because they had won their season series with the Athletics and Boston.

If none of this legislation had been put through behind Chicago's back and the standings prior to the meeting had been retained, the White Stockings would still have earned the title because they won their season series with Philadelphia. The protests stressing these points lodged by the Chicago management later that fall and winter availed them nothing. The Athletics had stolen the 1871 title, and that was that.

A few clever writers have blamed Mrs. O'Leary's cow for the White Stockings blowing the 1871 pennant. It made good copy, but Ol' Bossy didn't do it. The pennant was stolen from them by Henry Chadwick and the eastern clubs at the fall meeting. They just couldn't stand seeing a western team win the national title for the third straight year, so they rigged the rules to fit their purpose. Chicago was cheated out of a second straight national championship, then some writers and historians who were enamoured with Chadwick made Mrs. O'Leary's cow the goat for it.

All things considered, the year of 1871 was quite remarkable for the Chicago White Stockings. They moved into a brand new park in the spring, played a good brand of baseball for the most part, won a title on the field, then saw all of it go up in smoke.

6

The Chicago Phoenix

The city of Chicago would rise again. Of that, there was no doubt. But how long would the recovery take? That was the question.

By the spring after *The Great Chicago Fire*, Chicagoans were in full swing rebuilding the Garden City. New and better buildings were rising where fire—traps had once stood. Money was pouring into the city in spite of the number of insurance companies that had been bankrupted by the disaster. Chicago would live again and attain even greater glory than before.

As for baseball, Chicago *Tribune* editor and publisher Joseph Medill, one of the founders of the Chicago Base Ball Club, wrote an editorial calling for the club's management to forego any plans to re—establish the team. Medill said 1872 was too soon after the great fire for Chicagoans to be thinking about leisurely pastimes; they had a city to rebuild and that should be their only priority.

Not everyone saw things the way Medill did.

At the first meeting of the Chicago Base Ball Club after the fire, Secretary Ed Thacher reported that all the club's papers, records, and cash had been destroyed when the fire burned down the club house, grandstands, and fences at Union Grounds. To make matters worse,

Thacher said that the insurance company could only pay the club 10 cents on the dollar on their policy; meaning the club would receive $400 for its loss instead of $4,000.

In spite of this gloom, several members of the Chicago Base Ball Club came together in early April 1872 and made plans to field a team that would henceforth be known as the Phoenix Base Ball Club of Chicago. Officers were elected, and a new constitution was drawn up because the old one had been destroyed in the fire. Then the split came.

Some stockholders felt securing a playing field should be their priority, while others argued that they needed a team before they needed a park. The team notion was quickly put down as impractical because the players that had been signed the year before had been given their releases and were already under contract to other teams. Then an amateur nine would have to make do, was the retort; but few wanted to back a bunch of amateurs; that had been tried and had failed. Those favoring getting up a team were outvoted, and plans were laid to find a suitable place to build a new park. Disgusted, the stockholders supporting the team idea left the meeting in a huff and decided to go it alone. They took the name of the Phoenix Base Ball Association of Chicago and tried to field a nine that year but failed.

In the meantime, the other stockholders temporarily resumed the use of the Chicago Base Ball Club for the name of their organization, and they went about the business of electing officers and securing a piece of real estate for a playing field. Norman Gassette and Ed Thacher were voted in as president and secretary again. The land for a park was found at what became 23rd and State streets on the Southside. The club took what meager funds it could muster, rented the site from the city, then built a new park that was the envy of the nation at that time.

Since almost everyone in Chicago was tapped out because of the fire, it was decided that it would be a futile gesture to attempt to raise more capital through stock subscriptions, especially since Medill openly opposed any such effort in the pages of the *Tribune*. Therefore, a motion was made and passed to rent out the new playing field to any and all comers until such time as enough revenue was realized to retain the services of a pro nine once more.

It took the Chicago Base Ball Club almost two full summers to come up with enough rents to hire a dozen professional players for a team that would suit up in 1874. Much of the money was raised by eastern clubs that came to Chicago to play some of their games during the seasons of 1872 and 1873.

With the rents as seed money, the stockholders reorganized yet again. The first thing they did was change the name of the club to the Chicago Base Ball *Association*, and a new charter was granted to them by the state in the summer of 1873. Gassette and Thacher were again elected as the two officers, and business proceeded as usual.

The first man hired by the Chicago Base Ball Association was former White Stockings captain Jimmy Wood, who had split the 1872 season between the Brooklyn Eckfords and the Troy Haymakers and had played in '73 for the Philadelphia Club (not the Athletics) whose team had appropriated the nickname of White Stockings.*

* In most books on the subject, the Philadelphia Club is

Thinking to save money and consolidate authority, Gassette gave the managerial reins to Wood instead of rehiring Tom Foley to manage the club.

As both captain (field manager) and (general) manager, Wood then went about the business of hiring a team for the 1874 season. He was able to convince Ned Cuthbert, Levi Meyerle, Fred Treacy, George Zettlein, and Ed Pinkham to rejoin the Chicago squad.

Treacy, Meyerle, and Cuthbert had spent the last two years in Philadelphia, playing for the Athletics in '72 and the Philly White Stockings in '73. Pinkham had remained in Chicago, playing for various amateur teams, and Zettlein had followed his pal Wood to Troy, Brooklyn, and Philadelphia.

Joining this sextet of returning Whites were Jimmy Devlin, Davy Force, John Glenn, Paul Hines, and Fergy Malone.

Devlin was in his second year as a pro and had been whisked away from the Philadelphia White Stockings by Wood.

Force started his NA pro career with the Washington Olympics in '71, then joined Wood on the Troy Haymakers until that club folded in the middle of the '72 campaign, going to the Lord Baltimore Club of Baltimore after that, staying with the Canaries through '73.

Glenn was Force's teammate in Washington in '71, then left the Olympics when they folded in early '72 for the Washington Nationals, playing through the end of

referred to as the *Philadelphias* instead of as the Philadelphia White Stockings. This was probably to avoid confusing them with the Chicago nine. Also, the Philadelphia press used the name because the team had so many former Chicago players on it.

the '73 season for the Nats.

Hines, who was totally deaf, played with Glenn for the Nationals in '72 and '73 before Wood talked him into coming to Chicago for the '74 season.

Malone was an Irish immigrant who caught for the Philadelphia Athletics for years before jumping to the Philadelphia Club's White Socks in '73.

Lewis Meacham bragged mightily in the pages of the Chicago *Tribune* about Chicago's new '74 team, going so far as to call them Giants, possibly with the intent of changing their nickname. Fortunately, Giants didn't catch on. Later in the year he would rue his ill–advised fit of braggadocio.

Early in 1874, Jimmy Wood took a fall in his home and severely bruised a leg. The contusion refused to heal and gradually developed into an abscess that also defied medical treatment. Because of this condition, Wood was confined to bed by the doctors. He was still bedridden when the players reported for spring practice in March.

Since Wood couldn't run the team, George Zettlein was made acting–captain of the nine on the field, and Nicholas Young was hired to run the team off the field.

Young had managed the Washington Olympics before they folded, and he was the secretary of the National Association, having held that post since the NA's inception. He was also one of the finest umpires in the country and was considered to be totally honest and knowledgeable of the game by the players, managers, and newspaper scribes alike.

Young and Zettlein led the White Stockings south for a series of exhibitions against amateur nines in St. Louis during late April. Three weeks later Zettlein opened the pro season by shutting out the Philadelphia Athletics by a 4–0 score, and there was joy in Chicago as baseball devotees felt certain the whip pennant would fly over the Windy City once again.

The glee didn't last long. After dropping the next two games, Ed Pinkham hung up his spikes, and Johnny Peters, an infielder who had played outstandingly for the St. Louis Reds when the Whites visited the River City for a few exhibitions earlier in the year, was signed to replace the departing lefty.

Other players were shifted to different positions, and Levi Meyerle was benched with a sore shoulder. Jimmy Wood was getting better but was still confined to his bed.

As the first day of summer rolled up on the calendar, the Whites' situation hadn't changed much. Chicago was playing .500 ball and was apparently going no where without their first line captain. To add to the Chicago Base Ball Association's hassles, city Alderman Cullerton proposed a ticket tax for the White Stockings' games. The *Tribune* led the chorus of condemnations and called upon voters in his district to reject his re–election bid that fall. Cullerton's proposal failed with the city council, and he struck out at the polls in November.

As if things weren't bad enough on the home front, the White Stockings were faced with troubles on the road, too. When they arrived in New York, Zettlein and Ned Cuthbert were accused of being in the pay of gamblers and of throwing several games. Until the charges were investigated thoroughly, both men were forced to sit out the New York contests, which the White Stockings lost, much to the delight of the New York *Herald*'s baseball writer who derisively called the Whites the *Chicago Giants*. As soon as the last game was played, both players were conveniently exonerated of all charges and permitted to resume their careers. In Chicago, this became known as New York justice.

Nothing seemed to be going right for the Chicago nine. Early in July the Whites were mired in fifth place, four games under .500, and more than a dozen games behind the England–bound Boston Red Stockings. Being so vulnerable to criticism, the St. Louis *Globe* decided the *White Socs* were in a weak enough spot to poke a little fun at them:

> The Chicago Base Ball Club has hired two players at Easton, Pa. The great "Chicago Nine" now consists of four Philadelphians, two Eastonians, two St. Louisans, and one Baltimorean. The President, however, is a Chicagoan, and so, we are given to under–stand, is one of the ticket–sellers at the gate. All of which recalls to the unprejudiced mind the "revolutionary musket." A new lock, a modern stock, and a naval barrel had been substituted as the hallowed old ones wore out, "but," said the proprietor, reverently, but with enthusiasm, "darn ye, the touch–hole is revolutionary."

Then the worst happened.

The abscess on Jimmy Wood's leg finally healed in early July, and the doctor said it would be all right for him to get out of bed and move around on a pair of crutches. Having spent the better part of six months on his back, Wood eagerly slipped the walking aids under his arms and pushed himself upright. The sudden rush of blood to his stiff leg was painful at first, but the discomfort gradually subsided. As soon as it did, he tried to put a little weight on the limb and lost his balance for the briefest of moments. The room was filled with a loud cracking noise, and Wood collapsed in more agony than one man should ever feel. Both bones in his lower leg were shattered, broken in multiple places and totally beyond repair by medical standards of the day. Apparently, the abscess had affected the bones, making them extremely brittle. The doctors only had one course of action. On July 11, it was reported that Jimmy Wood, age 29, had a leg amputated, bringing a tragic end to the playing career of the first Chicago Cub.

Four days after the *Tribune* reported Wood's operation Chicago was struck by the second worst fire in its history. On July 15, 19 square blocks of the city's center went up in flames.

Included in the blaze was the ball park at 23rd and State streets. The Whites lost their home but not their equipment this time. They moved their remaining home games to Ogden Park and continued play. The ticket offices were moved to Kelley Bros., at 88 Madison Street and 117 22nd Street.

Wood's good friend George Zettlein rallied the team by asking them to dedicate the remainder of the season to their fallen captain. By July 28 when a benefit exhibition was played for Jimmy Wood, it looked like they just might do that, climbing back to two games over .500 and moving into third place in front of the New York Mutes who were due into town.

The Mutuals had defeated the White Stockings two straight in New York earlier in the year as their ace pitcher, Bobby Mathews, was enjoying the best year of his career against Chicago. New York won the first two games in Chicago behind the masterly arm of Mathews, and it appeared he would do it again in the third contest.

With the Mutes leading the Whites, Mathews left the game at the end of the fifth inning, claiming illness as his reason for leaving. Chicago fought back and pulled out a 5–4 victory, but as soon as the game ended, New York's catcher, the famous Doug Allison, started screaming that Mathews had thrown the game by leaving in the middle of it.

A big argument ensued as the local newspaper reporters gathered around Allison like so many vultures circling over a dying horse in the desert. Allison told them that Mathews had been hanging around with a well known gambler named McDonald and that McDonald had visited New York captain Tom Carey at the Mutuals' hotel the night before. The newspapermen put on their detective clothes and went sleuthing about town.

The journalists earned their pay that week. They learned that McDonald and another gambler had placed a few bets with their good friend Tom Foley, the same man who had been the business manager for the White Stockings in years past and who ran a betting parlor and billiards hall in his saloon and whose reputation for honesty was so great that he was often sought after to umpire in the Chicago area. Their total winnings at Foley's was less than $50 — hardly an amount to raise suspicion.

Then Alexander V. Davidson, the Mutuals' manager, said that Mathews had been under a physician's care since the evening of the previous game with the White Stockings. Corroborating Davidson's statement was an affidavit issued by Dr. A.J. Baxter, M.D., specifically stating that he had been caring for Mathews for two days prior to the game under suspicion. When he was questioned about the incident, Tom Foley said that he knew about Mathews' illness before the game but that he hadn't told anyone because he knew it would upset the betting. Without Mathews, the Mutuals were no longer superior to the White Stockings, only equal to them; and this would cause bettors to stay away from the parlors.

Although the end result of the affair was that Mathews was cleared of any wrongdoing, there was much talk around town about relations between New Yorkers and Chicagoans. The *Tribune* had something to say concerning the entire episode:

> Like all New Yorkers, they believe that there is nothing worthy of consideration beyond the confines of Manhattan Island, and they treat us Western people as if we were a community of idiots, of whom any advantage may be taken without danger of discovery.

Odd, isn't it, that the same attitude between New Yorkers and Midwesterners was to prevail for generations yet to come?

Within that month of August 1874, five Philadelphia players — John Radcliff, William "Candy" Cummings, Nat Hicks, Denny Mack, and Bill Craver (remember him?) — were charged with throwing games at the urging of gamblers. An investigation was held, and it was determined that only Radcliff had done anything illegal when he attempted to bribe umpire Bill McLean. Radcliff was then banished from the club but was back playing pro ball the next season with another team.

The Chicago Base Ball Association held its annual meeting in August that year, and George Gage and William Ambrose Hulbert were elected president and secretary, respectively, of the club. The first thing Gage did was replace Nick Young with Jimmy Wood who was finally up and around on crutches. Wood then replaced Zettlein as captain by giving the title, but not the ac–companying responsibilities, to Malone. Wood took the team's reins and became the *first non-playing* field manager.

Although the Mutuals got close once, Harry Wright's Boston Red Stockings won their third straight National Association flag. The White Stockings finished a distant fifth.

That fall, while he was trying to put together a winner for the 1875 season, Jimmy Wood was interviewed by Meacham about all the gambling that had gone on during the past year. Wood refused to be caught in a journalistic snare but did imply that all four New York and Phila–delphia teams had several crooked players. Only Boston had an honest team, and it was his goal to give Chicago an equally trustworthy nine for the coming year.

At the annual convention of the National Association on March 1, 1875, the rules committee made further changes in the way the game was played. No longer would it take three strikes to get a batter out at the plate; two would do. No longer could a batter let the first pitch go and not have it count for or against him. "Wides" were done away with, making every pitch either a ball or a strike. To speed up things a bit and settle a lot of arguments, the method of selecting umpires was changed. Visiting teams had to send the home team a list of five possible candidates — men who had nothing to do with the visitors — at least a week in advance of the game, and the home team had to respond by telegraph within 48 hours with its choice.

There was one more rule change that had a big effect on the game as it was played in the 1870s. The early rule concerning pitching stated simply that a pitcher had to toss the ball toward home plate, meaning propel it forward underhanded with his hand and arm as parallel to his side as possible. The regulation said nothing about how high he could swing his arm backward then forward. The hitters complained bitterly that pitchers were *whipping* the ball forward and not *tossing* it, but the umpires were powerless to do anything about it because the motion was within the rules. For 1875, the rule was amended to state that a pitcher's hand couldn't be raised above the line of his hip — not pelvis, but hip — while in the motion of tossing the ball toward the plate. Old style pitchers were delighted, and so were hitters.

During the off season, a serious problem arose concerning Davy Force. Little did anyone realize at the time, but Davy Force was the catalyst for a series of events that would change baseball forever.

The National Association's rules stated that a player couldn't be signed to a contract until his current team released him or his present agreement came to an end, whichever came first. Force signed a contract for '75 with the White Stockings in September '74. When it was realized that this contract wasn't valid, he signed another in November '74. The problem was it was backdated to September.

In December '74, Force determined that he would rather play for the Athletics in Philadelphia in '75, so he signed a contract with them because they told him his pact with the White Stockings was still invalid because it was dated in September.

At the winter convention, the argument between the

two teams over Force was put before the judiciary committee. Testimony was heard and evidence presented. The decision was that Force belonged to Chicago for '75 because the second contract had been signed in November and the September date meant nothing. Case closed, right?

Because of the Force case, the rules committee put through a new regulation that simply stated that a player couldn't sign with another team until he was either released or the current season came to an end, whichever came first. Good going, right?

As was done every year at the annual meeting of pro clubs, officers for the National Association were elected. In 1875, Charles Spering, an official with the Philadelphia Athletics, was voted in as president. His first act of office was to appoint a new judiciary committee with himself as chairman and representatives from each of the other Philadelphia teams — the Pearls and the Centennials — and one each from New York and Hartford. He then reopened the Force case under the new rules and by a vote of 4–0 with one abstention gave Force to the Athletics.

The Chicagoans, led by William Hulbert, screamed their indignation at this travesty of justice, and they were supported by all the other western clubs as well as Boston in the East.

For all it was worth, Force played for the Athletics that year because nothing could be done without another convention to remove the high–handed Spering from office. Another national confab was out of the question, of course, what with the playing season already in progress by the time it could be arranged.

Jimmy Wood put together a decent nine for 1875 that

included Jimmy Devlin, Johnny Peters, John Glenn, Paul Hines, and George Zettlein back from the '74 squad. Joining them for the coming campaign were Scott Hastings, most recently of Hartford but with experience with Rockford in '71, the Baltimore Canaries and Cleveland in '72, and the Canaries again in '73; Oscar Bielaski, who had played for the Washington Olympics in '72 and '73, and the Canaries in '74; Dick Higham, the former captain of the Mutuals; Warren White, who had played in Washington for three years, 1871–73, then with the Canaries in '74; and George Keerl, the same man who had played for the White Stockings in 1870 then went to Canada to play. Wood made Higham the field captain, but he continued to manage the team from the bench.

The 1875 nine got off to a good start, playing the newest western entries in the baseball derby that year. The Whites took the measure of the Keokuk Westerns and St. Louis Reds with little trouble but were given fits by the St. Louis Browns and their topnotch pitcher George Washington Bradley. A few of the weaker eastern teams came to Chicago for a lesson in hardball, and by June 13, the Whites were 13–4, only two losses behind the mighty Boston Red Stockings.

Everything was going so well until the Chicago *Times* ran a story about Jimmy Wood accusing his old friend George Zettlein of throwing a game to Boston. Three days later the *Tribune* contradicted the rival paper with an interview of Wood by Meacham:

> Wood: ... I am very sorry that this statment in regard to George was published, because it will have a bad effect upon the Club. I don't see why the newspapers should be ever—

lastingly pitching into us when we do so much
for them.

Tribune : In what way?

Wood: There are thousands of people who
buy the papers simply for the reports of the
games, and who would not otherwise think of
looking at a newspaper.

Tribune : I believe that was true back in the
baseball times of 1870, but hardly think it is
correct now.

Wood: I should think it would be, since there is
quite as much excitement over base–ball now
as there was then. Of course, we don't object
to being criticised when we do anything that is
wrong, but I don't see why the newspapers
should be pitching into us all the time when
there is no cause for it. There seems to be a
sort of determination to run down the Club.

"Woodsey" – as his friends were now calling him be–
cause of his new wooden leg as well as because of his last
name — had the Fourth Estate figured out well enough,
but Meacham deserved to be congratulated for having
the courage and confidence to print Wood's criticism of
journalists.

The interview did little to help the White Stockings or
the National Association as it turned out. Zettlein asked
for and was given his release on August 3, citing mis–
treatment by Wood. Jimmy was astounded by the
charge, stating that he had given Zet every chance at
every turn. Woodsey was guilty of being too close to his
long–time friend. Zettlein then signed with the Phila–
delphia Club and was involved in a gambling scandal
there later in the season.

The direct result of the Zettlein affair was the removal of Higham as captain, the installation of John Glenn to that post, and a five-game losing streak that dropped the Whites into fifth place on Sunday July 4. It didn't make much difference though. The next day the '75 season was practically over for the Chicagoans — all things considered.

7

The Hulbert–Spalding (Mostly Hulbert) Conspiracy

Jimmy Wood made a good point about the newspapers doing their worst to hurt the White Stockings instead of helping them. Some writers — including Lewis Meacham of the *Tribune* — cried about every loss and acted like Vince Lombardi when he was asked if he ever praised his players and he responded, "I should pat them on the back for doing their jobs?"

There was more trouble at Chicago "and always would be as long as the press and public treat the nine so that no man of any self–respect can hold a position on it," was the opinion of the New York *Herald*:

> For if they win they are good fellows — but if they lose they are muffers and rascals. They are abused without stint unless they conquer every foe and the papers are determined to run the nine. When a newspaper such as the *Tribune* indulges in such abuse constantly it does an incalculable injury to any club.

But just maybe Chicago's daily rags weren't as useless as Wood and the eastern papers were saying.

After the White Stockings suffered their third straight loss in early July '75, T.Z. Cowles, the prominent reporter of the *Tribune* who had a permanently free seat in the press row at the ball park, started up his wailing machine and belittled Chicago's pro team with some of his best insults. Meacham countered Cowles by making a suspicious suggestion. He wrote that the White Stockings' management might be wise to contract the best of the '75 team for '76 right now, then start recruiting the best players in the National Association immediately. More than likely, Meacham, who was closer to club secretary William A. Hulbert than any other journalist in the city, might have only suspected something like this might be in the works, or he might have been privy to certain inside information and couldn't wait to get it into print.

Chicago's professional baseball organization had been undergoing changes ever since *The Great Chicago Fire*. Its name had been changed from Chicago Base Ball Club to Chicago Base Ball Association, and a new charter under that name had been registered with the state of Illinois in the summer of 1873. New faces had come into the management picture and were making their presence felt. Among them was the man who would reshape not only the destiny of the Chicago club but the future of professional baseball.

William Ambrose Hulbert was born on October 23, 1832 in Burlington Flats, New York, not far from Cooperstown. He came to Chicago at an early age with his family. He attended and graduated from Beloit College in Beloit, Wisconsin, then took a job as a clerk for a coal merchant in Chicago. Eventually, he married the boss's daughter and came to own the business. Soon enough, he was a member of the Board of Trade and a part of the social elite in the Garden City. Like most affluent men of his era, he was overweight — a sure sign of success! — and mustachioed, although he kept his whiskers confined to his upper lip. In personality and character, he was strong, forceful, self-reliant, and possessed a tremendous amount of energy, courage, and confidence but was far from being an ego-maniac. He was the kind of man who recognized a good deal when it jumped up in front of him then did something about it. Hulbert was a true capitalist who was pragmatic and forthright about everything, even to the point of believing that the end justified the almost any means.

Hulbert was an original subscriber to the stock of the Chicago Base Ball Association. When he became the secretary of that organization on August 19, 1874, he saw the White Stockings not as a sporting proposition but as a business venture. It wasn't hard for him to figure how easy it would be to make the club very profitable. The 1870 season had been the perfect example of this: put a winning nine of honest players on the field and the customers will buy tickets by the score. This was Hulbert's and club president George Gage's precise aim when they took control of the club in '74.

The rules of the National Association forbade any contact between the management of one team and a player of another, but there was nothing that the NA could do about it when it occurred between annual conventions as in the Davy Force case. When the NA could act, the worst punishment it could inflict would be to nullify any contracts and expel the club from the organization. The latter wasn't likely to happen to the White Stockings because the eastern clubs needed a strong team in the West. Bill Hulbert was well acquainted with the NA's impotence, having been the victim in the Force incident. The duplicity of Spering and the other eastern hucksters convinced him that Chicago and other western cities would never get an even break as long as the NA was run as it was; that is, by Easterners such as Spering. If professional baseball was to survive and thrive, it had to be run by honest men working with stricter rules.

Harry Wright and the Boston Red Stockings management had had the foresight and intelligence to prevent their players from revolving to other teams by signing them to three-year contracts whenever possible. Hulbert saw the good business sense in this method of dealing with players under the current condition of the NA and admired Wright for employing it.

Hulbert also knew that several of these players' agreements with the Boston club were due to expire at the end of the '75 season. The fact that some of these same players were from the West was the icing on the cake. The temptation of this knowledge was too much for Hulbert not to act accordingly.

Hulbert wasn't a man to buy a pig in a poke. He studied the backgrounds of the best players in the rest of the pro ranks and learned which of them were natives of the West or had at least grown up there. From this total group of Westerners, he pinpointed the one man who possessed the managerial ability, personal integrity, and leadership qualities to run a baseball team as a business. With revenge against Spering as his ilk for motivation, Hulbert made his move.

"You've no business playing in Boston; you're a Western boy, and you belong right here," Hulbert secretly wrote to Albert G. Spalding, Harry Wright's ace pitcher.* After telling him it was his duty to play in Chicago, Hulbert implied that the positions of captain and manager of the White Stockings for '76 would be available to Spalding if he was so inclined.

Young Al Spalding was more than inclined. Albert Goodwill Spalding was born September 9, 1850 in the small farming village of Byron, Illinois where his father was one of the more affluent citizens. The elder Spalding died in 1858, and in 1862, young Al was sent to Rockford to live with an aunt while he attended school. A year later the rest of his family — his mother, sister Mary, and brother James Walter — moved to the industrious little city on the Rock River. It was there that Spalding learned to play baseball, being asked to join a boys team simply because he could throw a ball farther than anyone already on the nine. As he grew and his skills improved, he was asked to become a member of the newly formed Forest City Club, which eventually became Rockford's town team and a professional organization.

Spalding first achieved national recognition when he was the winning pitcher in Rockford's victory over the seemingly invincible Washington Nationals in 1867. As the Forest Citys continued to defeat the best nines in the West, their reputation spread across the country. Harry Wright heard about them and scheduled a game between Rockford and his Cincinnati Red Stockings in 1869. Although the Reds won, Wright was impressed by Spalding's pitching. The next year when the Rockford nine made a tour of the East and defeated almost every

* Hulbert was one of the first baseball men to recognize that pitching is the most singularly important facet of the game, even in his day when the rules favored the hitters far more than the moundsmen.

team they faced, Wright decided he wanted Spalding pitching for him.

Wright signed Spalding to a Boston contract for the '71 season and each of the next four as Spalding became the game's premier hurler.

Early on in his playing career, Spalding realized that he couldn't play baseball forever and that sooner or later he would have to decide on what he intended to do with the rest of his life. This notion continued to haunt him even though he was being paid a fat salary by the Boston club that was three times the pay the average working man was earning annually. So he was continually wondering what he should do when his playing days were over. In Boston, he didn't have far to look for an idea.

Harry Wright and his brother George learned early on how to exploit their fame as athletes. It was Harry's talents as a cricket player that first took him to Cincinnati when the English game was all the rage. He was hired to teach the sport to an Ohio club, and it was while he was working at this job that Aaron Champion recognized Wright's leadership abilities and hired him to manage and captain the Cincinnati Red Stockings. When the Cincinnati club folded due to financial difficulties, some of which may have been deliberately caused by Wright, Harry and George moved to Boston and started their own club — but wisely with other people's capital. With their own funds, they went into the sporting goods business, putting their names on the sign out front which was practically all they had to do to make money.

Seeing what the Wrights had done in Boston wasn't enough for Spalding.* He had to prove to himself that he

---

* Spalding also had Al Reach as an example to follow.

could handle a business. Harry Wright gave him this chance in '74 when he put Spalding in charge of making the advance arrangements for the Red Stockings' tour of England and Ireland. Spalding handled these duties as well as any professional public relations director might. It was this newfound business acumen and his organizational abilities that inspired Spalding to realize that he could attain a higher position in life.

With this confidence in himself and the knowledge of the Wrights' success, Spalding conferred with his brother Walter about the two of them going into the sporting goods business, and together they decided they could do no less than Harry and George Wright but in another area, preferably some place in the West — like Chicago. It was practically home turf where Walter could mind the store, while Al promoted their concern by playing baseball.

Walter's consent to join him in the business venture pushed Spalding over the edge. He wrote back to Hulbert offering his services to the Chicago Base Ball Association for the '76 season.

At a meeting of the Chicago Base Ball Association's directorate — George Gage, Phillip Wadsworth, Charles S. Bartlett, E.F. Dexter, and Hulbert — held July 3, 1875 at Bartlett's residence, "Mr. Hulbert then read letter from A.G. Spalding of the Boston (Mass.) Base Ball Club offering his services as 'Manager' of our club for 1876. After careful consideration and discussion Mr.

Reach was an early professional player who capitalized on his fame by starting a sporting goods company in Philadelphia that survived him. Actually, Harry and George Wright followed his example.

Upper: Alexander Cartwright
Lower: Henry Chadwick

Upper: 1862 baseball game in progress above formation
       Fort Pulaski, Savannah, Georgia
Lower: 1862 baseball game in progress, Union prisoners
       playing at Salisbury, North Carolina

Above left: George Wright
Above right: Harry Wright
Lower: William Hulbert

Upper: 1869—Rockford "Forest
       Citys" featuring Spalding 3rd
       from right
Lower: 1870 Rockford team

Upper: 1870 Chicago White Stockings   Standing: Keerl,
      Duffy, Tracey, Hodes, Flynn, Cuthbert
      Seated: Meyerle, Pinkham, Wood, McAtee, King
Lower: 1871 Chicago White Stockings   Wood in center,
      clockwise from top, Simmons, Pinkham, McAtee,
      King, Foley, Zettlein, Atweter, Hodes, Duffy, Treacy

Upper left: A. G. Spalding, 1869
Upper right: A. G. Spalding, 1873
Lower left: A. G. Spalding, 1877
Lower right: A. G. Spalding, 1882

A. G. Spalding, 1886

Upper left: Cap Anson "Baby," 1871
Upper right: Cap Anson, 1873
Lower left: Cap Anson, 1875
Lower right: Cap Anson, 1877

Upper left: Cap Anson, 1880
Lower left: Cap Anson, 1885
Right: Cap Anson, 1876

Upper left: Mike "King" Kelly, 1874
Upper right: Mike "King" Kelly, 1878
Lower left: Mike "King" Kelly, 1882
Lower right: Mike "King" Kelly, 1886

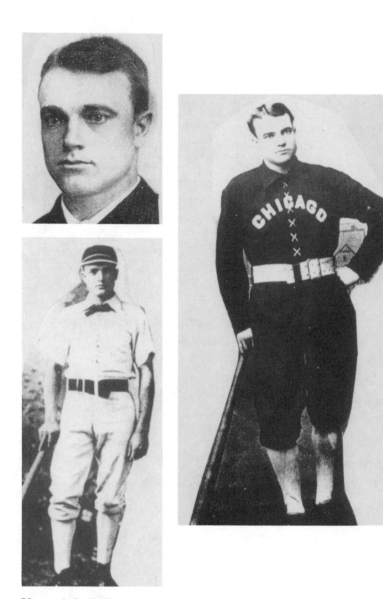

Upper left: Billy Sunday, 1881
Lower left: Billy Sunday, 1883
Right: Billy Sunday, 1886

Constitution.

Article I.   Name.

Name.

This association shall be called, The National League of Professional Base-Ball Clubs.

Article II.   Objects.

Objects.

The objects of this League are,

1. To encourage, foster and elevate the game of base-ball

2. To enact and enforce proper rules for the exhibition and conduct of the game:

3. To make base-ball playing respectable and honorable:

4. To protect and promote the mutual interests of professional base-ball clubs and professional base-ball players: and

5. To establish and regulate the "Base-Ball Championship of the United States"

Article III.   Membership.

Membership.

— This League shall consist of the following named Professional Base-Ball Clubs, namely:

Athletic B.B. Club of Philadelphia, Pa.;

Boston B.B. Club of Boston, Mass.;

Chicago B.B. Club of Chicago, Ills.;

Cincinnati B.B. Club of Cincinnati, Ohio;

Hartford B.B. Club of Hartford, Conn.;

Mutual B.B. Club of Brooklyn, N.Y.;

Louisville B.B. Club of Louisville, Ky.; and

St. Louis B.B. Club of St. Louis, Mo.,

and such other professional Clubs as may, from time to

1876 National League Constitution

Upper left: 1876 Chicago
White Stockings
Upper right: 1879 Chicago
White Stockings
Lower left: 1881 Chicago
White Stockings
Below: 1884 Chicago White
Stockings

Upper: 1885 team
Lower: 1886 Championship team; Top: Billy Sunday, Abner
      Dalrymple, Ned Williamson, Jimmy Ryan, Jocko
      Flynn, Tommy Burns; middle: King Kelly, George
      Gore, George Moolic, Fred Pfeffer, Silver Flint;
      bottom: John Clarkson, Cap Anson, Jim McCormick

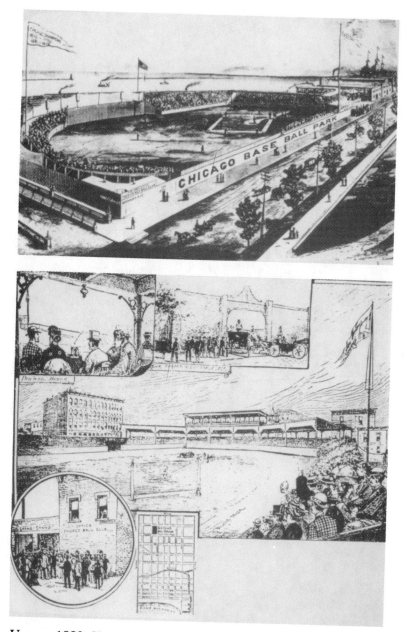

Upper: 1883 Chicago White Stockings Park
Lower: 1885 West Side Park

Chicago Championship team meets the President

Hulbert was instructed to visit Boston, and confirm the best arrangement possible with Mr. Spalding, and also to engage such players for the season of 1876 as he and Mr. Spalding should decided upon — "

Spalding initiated the contact? At least that's what the minutes of the meeting state. Of course, the minutes were kept by the club secretary, William A. Hulbert. No mention was made of the fact that Hulbert had initiated the contact with Spalding. If Hulbert told them this at the meeting, he failed to record it in the minutes. He probably didn't have to tell them about it if he was as close to these men as so much of the documented evidence suggests he was. They probably knew that Hulbert could be devious and secretive, especially if they had been privy to any of his correspondence.

According to a hearsay report of the meeting made by Spalding some years after the fact and after the demise of the participants, the directors balked at doing anything immediately. They felt they should let the matter rest until the appropriate time at the end of the season. Hulbert was beside himself. Here he had practically placed baseball's top pitcher at their feet and these horse–blindered executives were turning their backs on him. The club secretary quickly reminded them of the Force case and how they had been victimized by the conniving Easterners. Here was their chance to get even with them. After much cajoling, arguing, fist–pounding, and a tad of shouting, Hulbert finally got his point across; to his delight, they agreed it was time for Chicago to avenge itself on the dastardly Easterners.

The directors of the club then "instructed" their secretary to go to Boston immediately and "confirm the best arrangement possible with Mr. Spalding." He was "to engage such players for the season of 1876 as he and

113

Mr. Spalding should decide upon."

Hulbert would have done this anyway because his plans for the future went well beyond the board room of the Chicago Base Ball Association.

Ostensibly traveling to Boston as advance man for the team which was two days behind him, Hulbert left Chicago on July 5 and met with Spalding a few days later in *total secrecy*. The two men liked each other straight away. Spalding was partial to Hulbert's straight–from–the–shoulder approach, and Hulbert was delighted to deal with an honest (impressionable was more like it) young man; Spalding was only 25. They dickered over the terms of the contract, then struck a deal where Spalding would be paid a salary of $2,000 annually and 25% of the next season's gate receipts as pitcher, captain, and manager of the Chicago White Stockings of '76.

Back in Chicago, this suspicious line was buried in an article by Lewis Meacham in the *Tribune*:

> Taking the field early this year, Chicago will
> secure the best players.

How much did Meacham know? Was he spying on Hulbert? Was Hulbert tipping him? More than likely, Hulbert had let it drop that he was going east to start rounding up some new ballplayers for '76, and Meacham seized this tidbit and put it in the paper.

As soon as he put his name on the bottom line, Spalding surprised his new employer. Knowing that he would accept almost any contract that gave him the dual positions of captain and manager, Spalding had taken the liberty of talking to a few of his teammates about going to Chicago with him. Ross Barnes, Cal McVey,

James Henry "Orator Jim" O'Rourke, and James "Deacon" White* told Spalding that they were open to suggestions. Of the four, only McVey was from the West, coming from Iowa. Each of the others was born and raised in New York state.

Although delighted by Spalding's news, Hulbert was still cautious. He told Spalding to ask them for verbal commitments — as opposed to written agreements which were against the NA's rules and therefore wouldn't be valid in the NA. He got them from Barnes, McVey, and White. O'Rourke decided to take a wait–and–see attitude; wait and see what the Boston management had to offer him once it was found out that the others had agreed to sign on with Chicago.

Not stopping with raiding the Red Stockings, Hulbert went on to Philadelphia and spoke to Ezra Sutton and Adrian Anson of the Athletics. He knew that both of them were fed up with the shenanigans of the Philadelphia magnates. Sutton was from New York, and Anson's home ground was Marshalltown, Iowa. Both men verbally committed themselves to play for the White Stockings in '76.

Satisfied that he had what he wanted, Hulbert returned to Chicago, and he reported to his fellow directors at Dexter's Old Store on 22nd Street Friday evening July 16, 1875. The minutes tell the tale of the special "Meeting called to hear Hulbert's report."

> Hulbert stated to meeting that pursuant to instructions of Directory (Meeting July 3) he

* This was the same Deacon White who had revolved on the White Stockings when the club was formed in 1870.

115

had visited Boston, New York & Philadelphia.
That he had had a long and full conference
with Mr. A.G. Spalding — and that prelim-
inary Articles of Agreement were duly drawn
and signed by Spalding & Hulbert (acting in
behalf of the Association).   Viz — The
Association guarantees Mr. Spalding a salary
of Two thousand dollars for the Season of
1876 and in addition twenty–five per cent of
the net profits arriving from the business of
the Association for the Season of 1876 —
These provisions to be incorporated in the
general contract with said Spalding —   A
special or sub contract also to be made with
Spalding convenying (sic) thirty per cent of
the net profits arriving from the business of
the Assn. for 1876 —   The provisions of the
sub–contract it was agreed should be kept a
secret — i.e., no persons outside the directory
were under any circumstances to be made
aquainted (sic) with its provisions.   It was
further agreed that Mr. Spalding should by
the Directory of the Assn. be duly elected
"Manager" and that his term of Office should
be from Nov. 1st 1875 to Nov. 15th 1876. The
understanding and agreement with Mr.
Spalding — and Mr. Hulbert as representative of the Association promised in behalf of
his fellow Directors that the same should in
good faith be carried out was that Spalding
was to have charge of and conduct in his own
person, all the detail business of the Association — The Supervision of the Directory to
be general — It being, of course, understood

that the Directory should have full control of the general policy of the club — but they are expected to act as a body and not in their individual capacity — The following named players were also engaged by Mr. Hulbert:

Mr. Roscoe C. Barnes   Salary $2,000
   and twenty–five per cent net
   profits business of the Assn
   season 1876 —

Calvin A. McVey   Salary   2,000
   Contract for two years from
   Nov 1, '75 — salary payable
   Monthly —

Jas. White   Salary   2,400
   $100 Additional provided club
   proves financial success

Adrian C. Anson   Salary   2,000
   $50 paid in cash $150 to be paid
   when regulier (sic) contract signed

Ezra B. Sutton   Salary   2,000
   $50 paid in cash $350 in
   installments during winter

Jno. P. Peters   Salary   1,500

   The foregoing is a fair transcript of what Mr. Hulbert said and his action is approved by us, and we hereby ratify & confirm the same.
(Signed)
Chas. S. Bartlett
E.F. Dexter
Geo. W. Gage
Philip Wadsworth

This was all supposed to be very hush–hush. The National Association had its rules to obey, didn't it? And these were men of unquestionable integrity, weren't they? Besides, there was the current season to consider. If word were to leak out about half of Boston's team as well as the Athletics' top two stars defecting to Chicago for '76, attendance would drop in every NA city and the National Association of Professional Base Ball Players would be ruined.

Top secret or not, Meacham blew the lid off the story on July 20 in the *Tribune*, reporting that Spalding, White, McVey, Barnes, O'Rourke, and Sutton were under contract and were coming to Chicago for '76 and that Devlin, Hines, Peters, Glenn, Golden, and Warren White were already retained from the '75 team. As if this wasn't enough to shock the toddling baseball world of 1875, the story went on to state that Harry and George Wright were so overwhelmed by the loss of five star players that they were disbanding the Boston club and returning to Cincinnati to start anew or retire from base-ball altogether.

The truth was only Spalding had signed anything, and that was a contract post–dated for the end of the current season in order to conform with the current National Association rules. Hulbert didn't want another Force case. All the others had only made verbal commitments or no commitment at all. As for the Wrights, they didn't know anything about the deals Spalding and Hulbert had made at this early date until Deacon White divulged this information at a dinner honoring the Red Stockings on the same evening that Meacham's story appeared in the *Tribune* a thousand miles away.

As soon as Harry did learn about it, he confronted his players, asking them how much the Chicagoans had offered. Spalding refused to reveal the terms of his contract, saying he was committed and no amount of money would sway him from the course he had already set for himself. Then speaking for the others, Spalding informed Wright of the numbers involved. Harry let out a low whistle, then wished them luck in Chicago because there was no way the Red Stockings could afford to meet those "fancy Western prices."

Learning of Wright's decision not to attempt to lure them back into the fold with more money, White, McVey, and Barnes signed contracts with Spalding. On the same day that Wright was losing the nucleus of his championship team for good, the *Tribune* made the announcement that Adrian Anson had verbally committed himself to be in a White Stockings' uniform in '76.

With each passing day, baseball devotees in the Garden City continued to gloat over Hulbert's *coup de grace*, while the fans in Boston and Philadelphia mourned the losses of their best players. The wailing in the eastern newspapers was quite verbose in spite of rumors that Spering and his bunch would do something to stop the Chicago pirates, just as they had with Davy Force.

Of course, not everything in Chicago was peaches and cream; some of the current version of the White Stockings were totally demoralized, starting with "The Charmer", George Zettlein, and Dick Higham. If they weren't throwing games before, Hulbert gave them good reason to do it after signing Spalding, et al, then letting it leak out that only a few of the present team would be in Chicago again in '76. Two weeks after Zettlein resigned and gained his release from the club, Higham was expelled and released for throwing games. The Whites didn't win many games either, even when Zettlein and Higham weren't throwing them. They were so bad that the local papers started calling them the *Giants*;

facetiously, of course.

All sorts of rumors began flying around baseball circles throughout the country. Every newspaper in the land had its own accounts of what had transpired, what was ongoing, and what the future had in store for various clubs and players. One such rumor stated that the New York Mutuals would be disbanding at the end of the season. The same was being said of the Philadelphia Athletics, what with Sutton and Anson leaving. Boston was also supposed to be on the rocks. Then there were the new clubs in Cincinnati and Louisville that were forming. The papers had them signing up all sorts of talent to meet the "menace" of Chicago.

As summer turned into fall, no one really knew what was going on except that sly fox Bill Hulbert who was quickly learning the value of the press as a business tool. Hulbert had seen how leaking an untrue story (such as the ones Tom Foley had spread in 1870 when he was trying to hire the best team available) could keep the newspapers and the public occupied while the real story had time to unfold in a natural order. He also recognized that the press could be used as a sounding board for his own ideas. When he let it out that the White Stockings were already considering signing new players for '76 as early as June of '75, he waited for public reaction as expressed in the papers, and when there was no negative response, he proceeded with his plans.

Like anyone with a good business head who cared anything about professional baseball, Hulbert realized that the National Association was no longer a viable entity for the sport. Changes were needed, especially in the power structure; western teams could no longer tolerate the abuses by certain eastern officials, such as Spering and his Philadelphia crowd. As soon as organ–

izations in Louisville and Cincinnati announced their plans to field professional nines for the 1876 season, Hulbert began corresponding with their leaders, letting them know where he stood as far as the NA was concerned.

By early October, it was obvious that he had gained some important allies for the future, and the St. Louis *Globe–Democrat* reported as fact that the St. Louis Browns, Chicago White Stockings, Cincinnati, and Louisville had formed a western clique with the express intention of doing something to break up the monopoly of the NA by the management of the Philadelphia Athletics and putting an end to the practices of such teams as the Brooklyn Atlantics, Washington Olympics, Washington Nationals, New Haven, and St. Louis Reds, all of which didn't make their road trips to the other sections of the country in '75 for various reasons.

When the public reaction to this news was favorable, Hulbert went a step further.

The baseball playing season was coming to an end, and the Boston Red Stockings were close to being named champions of the NA for the fourth consecutive year. Although they had signed contracts or made commitments to play in Chicago in '76, Spalding, McVey, Barnes, and White played harder than ever, just to prove to everyone that they weren't quitters but were honorable men living up to their contracts with the Boston club. Attendance for Boston's games, instead of dropping off as might have been expected, actually improved, thereby lending support to Hulbert's theory that the public wanted to see honest men playing the game on the up–and–up and would come out in large numbers to support teams that gave a complete effort to win. This was made equally apparent by the lack of attendance in

Chicago where the White Stockings had dismissed dishonest players in the latter half of the season and where the White Stockings came up croppers again in '75, finishing sixth with a record of 30–37.

With these facts behind him, Hulbert let it be known to Meacham — off the record, of course — that something would be done about the NA's "regulators (gamblers and players who conspired with the gamblers) and quitters (clubs) that didn't fulfill their contracts with other clubs" of '75. In the first place, the Brooklyn Atlantics weren't really a pro nine. They had used 38 different players that season, and they failed to play one game outside of the New York City area. Topping it off, they were a co-operative club. The St. Louis Reds were no better than the Atlantics, not playing any games east of Chicago. New Haven was too poorly capitalized to afford travel outside of the East, and the Washington teams were in the same boat.

Already in mid–October 1875, 17 clubs had announced that they intended to pay the $10 fee for the pursuit of the NA flag in '76. A half dozen of these were the financially strong teams of Chicago, St. Louis Browns, New York Mutuals, Hartford, Boston, and Philadelphia Athletics, and two more were the new entries from the West, Cincinnati, and Louisville, which had solid businessmen backing them with plenty of bucks to last an entire season. All the rest had problems, either with their finances or with their management's credibility.

When the leadership of the Chicago Base Ball Association failed to curtail the gambling activities of some players, meaning Zettlein and Higham, Hulbert became absolutely livid about the situation. At a stockholders meeting held Saturday night August 15, 1874, he called for President Norman T. Gassette* and the other officers of the club to resign — which they did. Hulbert was then elected to a board of directors pro tem that was to run the club for the remainder of the year. Hulbert didn't think that was such a good idea, so he called a stockholders meeting to "be held at Room No. 5   168 Randolph St. on Tuesday afternoon at 3:30 o'clock August 18th at which time a full board of Directors will be elected." Hulbert's demand for new leadership in the club polarized the membership, and a power struggle ensued between Hulbert and Gassette.

Never exactly a friend to Hulbert, Gassette attended the meeting with the intention of putting Hulbert and his faction in their proper place. Gassette started by challenging Gage's right to vote 10 shares of stock when Gage had only paid for five. Much to Gassette's surprise, Hulbert agreed. Hulbert countered by having the unpaid for five shares withdrawn from the club's total. Gassette then tried to have two of his cronies put on the new board of directors, while supporting Gage for the same position, thereby surprising his rival. When the votes were counted, Hulbert was unanimously elected, receiving 52 of the 52 votes cast. Also elected were Hulbert's buddies: E.F. Dexter, 44 votes; Philip Wadsworth, 42 votes; Gage, 39 votes; and Charles Bartlett, 34 votes. The losers were Thomas Courtney and Louis Viele, Gassette's pals. Gassette's support in the poll was a compromise in which Hulbert offered to back Gage for president. Figuring he could control the malleable Gage and thus the club, Gassette offered no

* In Hulbert's minutes and financial records for the club, he spelled Gassette's name Gazette.

more opposition that night. He didn't count on Hulbert getting elected secretary.

From that point, the Chicago Base Ball Association was slowly pulled out of the mire by Hulbert, although Gage was given most of the credit.

Hulbert was still doing his behind the scenes work when his plans were given an unexpected jolt by the untimely passing of George Gage, president of the Chicago Base Ball Association. Gage died of a stroke on September 24, 1875, supposedly leaving the White Stockings without a leader. Gage had been a very popular executive with the stockholders of the club, especially since *he had led* the organization out of chaos in '74. The truth was Gage was merely a figurehead. The real power behind the throne had belonged to William Ambrose Hulbert, having been his since the time he quietly seized it and maneuvered Gage to the top spot in the club.

After a respectable period of mourning, Hulbert called the club's stockholders together on October 10 and announced that he had received a proxy from Gage's widow for the late president's five shares of stock. This gave Hulbert control of voting rights for 39 shares of stock; more than enough to do as he wished with the club. He wished to be president, so he resigned as secretary and was duly elected to the top office. He wished to have Al Spalding on the board of directors and as secretary of the club. He got both at the same meeting. He had more wishes, but first a little groundwork had to be done.

On October 24, Hulbert used Lewis Meacham to boldly suggest in the *Tribune* that the six clubs that were financially sound and the new ones in Cincinnati and Louisville should be the only teams to compete for the NA's whip pennant in '76. Of course, the other nine so—

called pro teams would object to such a move; therefore, the reporter proposed the formation of a new association consisting of the strong clubs and operating under some new rules:

> (1) The new loop should only accept organiz-ations that could prove their financial backing was sound.
>
> (2) No club could be from a city of less than 100,000 population with the exception of Hartford because it was already a proven commodity.
>
> (3) No two clubs could be from the same city, such as the two then three Philadelphia nines.
>
> (4) A deposit of $1,000 or $1,500 should be made by each club with the association authorities at the beginning of each season as bond against their word that they would obey the rules and play all their games as scheduled.

The *Tribune* article wasn't well received around the country. Only the New York *Evening Post* editors had the sense to realize that some sort of reorganization of the NA was absolutely necessary to save professional baseball from becoming a circus sideshow. Henry Chadwick, the self–styled "Father of the Game", said Meacham's suggestions were too extreme and things weren't as bad as portrayed in Joe Medill's Chicago rag. The Philadelphia papers mocked the *Tribune*'s attempt to "destroy the Association;" if Chicago didn't like the way the NA was being run, she could jump in the lake. The Boston *Globe* complained that first Chicago stole all the best players in the East and now she wanted to steal the whole Association. Surprisingly, the Cincinnati and Louisville papers were silent on the subject, and the St. Louis tabloids were taking a wait–and–see attitude.

The ridicule by Chadwick and the other members of the eastern press only confirmed yet another Hulbert theory that the East was so entrenched in its belief that nothing good could come from west of the Allegheny Mountains that it wasn't about to accept change without a fight. To make certain he was right, Hulbert used Meacham to throw yet another gauntlet into the ring.

On November 21, another article appeared in the *Tribune* that supported the previous story of October 24. Since Chadwick and the Easterners thought so much of themselves, maybe the western clubs should go their own way and form a "Western Union" of professional clubs from Chicago, St. Louis, Cincinnati, Louisville, Indianapolis, Milwaukee, Cleveland, and Buffalo. Meacham proposed that since Harry Wright was apparently the only honorable man in the East that he join the honest magnates of the West and move his team to Indianapolis.

Chadwick politely mocked the *Tribune* again, saying professional baseball in the West would die without the eastern clubs coming to visit them each year, insinuating that the western teams needed the Easterns for drawing cards, then citing certain statistics that backed his theory. The *Tribune* responded with yet more numbers to support its contention that the best draw for all the eastern clubs in '74 and '75 had been the Chicago White Stockings; thereby, turning the tables on Chadwick.

Hulbert, for his part, decided it was time to keep the press out of his plans and put into action the master plan he had been developing since Spering and the Philadelphia gang had deprived the White Stockings of Davy

Force.* He and Spalding contacted the leaders of the other three western clubs and asked for a meeting to be held in Louisville. They all agreed to attend, then met in the Kentucky city on December 16–17. For two days, they hashed out their plans to rebuild the National Association or, if necessary, bolt from it and begin anew.

Just as it had been outlined in the *Tribune* in October, Hulbert proposed an eight–team league that would be bound by strict rules of organization and play that would also have decisive punishments for those who disobeyed. At the close of the meeting, the owners of the Louisville and Cincinnati clubs gave their powers–of–attorney to Hulbert and Charles A. Fowle of the St. Louis Browns to represent them at a meeting with the owners and representatives of four specified eastern clubs in the near future for the purpose of joining the four western clubs in a new organization to be known as the *National League of Professional Base–Ball Clubs*.

Fowle and Hulbert then drafted a letter which appeared in the *Tribune* in the following form a month after copies of it were mailed to the four eastern magnates they had in mind as necessary to create Hulbert's new league and a month after the meetings it proposed had taken place:

> St. Louis, Jan. 23. — The undersigned have been appointed by the Chicago, Cincinnati, Louisville, and St. Louis Clubs a committee to confer with you on matters of interest to the game at large, with special reference to the

* Hulbert wrote to Nicholas Apollonio, the president of the Boston Red Stockings, in April 1875, saying, "I want to raise the devil some way." He mentioned

reformation of existing abuses, and the formation of a new association, and we are clothed with full authority in writing from the above named clubs to bind them to any arrangement we may make with you. We therefore invite your club to send a representative clothed with like authority to meet us at the Grand Central Hotel, in the City of New York, on Wednesday, the 2d day of February next, at 12 m. After careful consideration of the needs of the professional clubs, the organizations we represent are of the firm belief that existing circumstances demand prompt and vigorous action by those who are the natural sponsors of the game. It is the earnest recommendation of our constituents that all past troubles and differences be ignored and forgotten, and that the conference we propose shall be a calm, friendly, and deliberate discussion, looking solely to the general good of the clubs who are calculated to give character and permanency to the game. We are confident that the propositions we have to submit will meet with your approval and support, and we shall be pleased to meet with you at the time and place above mentioned.

Yours respectfully,

W.A. Hulbert, Chas. A. Fowle

several ways of getting back at Spering and the other eastern clubs who supported him. The general tone of the letter said plainly that Hulbert wouldn't rest until he had avenged himself on the Easterners who had treated his beloved Chicago so shabbily.

Hulbert and Fowle weren't exactly operating in complete secrecy. Although they didn't inform their own cities' newspapers of what was afoot, neither did they ask the recipients of their missive to refrain from making notice of the upcoming meeting public. Fortunately for posterity, these men had the good sense to keep the conference clandestine.

At the appointed date, time, and place, Hulbert and Fowle met with Harry Wright and Nicholas T. Apollonio of the Boston Red Stockings; Morgan G. Bulkeley of Hartford; George W. Thompson (who replaced the dishonored Charles Spering as president of the club) and Messrs. Beach and Cragin of the Philadelphia Athletics; and William H. Cammeyer of the New York Mutuals. Harry Wright acted as secretary for the meeting.

Hulbert didn't beat around the bush. Quickly, he outlined his reasons for forming a new organization:

> (1) Get rid of bad elements, meaning players and managers who dealt with the gamblers or who drank excessively and let it interfere with their play.
>
> (2) Get rid of teams with bad management, meaning teams that were improperly capitalized, that were calling themselves professional but were actually semi-pro or co-operative clubs.
>
> (3) Self-preservation; get rid of clubs that wouldn't or couldn't play road games in the other section of the country.

Hardly pausing for breath, he reached into his coat pocket and withdrew a prepared constitution and by-laws — drawn up by Campbell Orrick Bishop, a lawyer from St. Louis — to govern the new National League of Professional Base–Ball Clubs. Cloaked in all the legal language of the day, these documents contained these points:

(1) Entrance fee per club would be $100 instead of $10.

(2) No club in a city with less than 75,000 population or within five miles of another NL city could join.

(3) No NL club could play a non–NL team in an NL city.

(4) Board of five directors to run league; each club to have one vote; board to elect president but secretary–treasurer to be hired and can't belong to any of the clubs in the NL.

(5) A club was permitted to sign a player for the coming year at any time, then the league office had to be notified immediately so the secretary could notify all the other clubs who were then to keep their hands off; but if a player signed a contract with one team after signing with another, he and the second team would be expelled from the NL.

(6) Players released from one club couldn't sign with another until the league office was notified that his character was okay and 20 days had passed.

(7) Teams were to play each other 10 times — five home and five away — for a total of 70 games to be played between March 15 and November 15.

Morgan G. Bulkeley of Hartford was elected the first

president of the National League after Hulbert turned down the office, and Nicholas Young, the former manager of the Chicago White Stockings, was hired as the first secretary–treasurer.

There were also some minor playing rule changes concerning fouls and base running, but nothing more of significance transpired at the meeting.

Before adjournment, the representatives of all eight clubs signed the documents, and the National League of Professional Base–Ball Clubs was born.

8

Spalding's Champions

"Those who complain about the way the ball bounces are usually the ones who dropped it." This anonymous quote could have been made the week after the National League was formed.

Although the New York and Philadelphia newspapers generally praised Hulbert and the other gentlemen who united in common cause, New Haven's tabloid and Henry Chadwick complained bitterly and for the same reason: both were left out.

The National Association of Professional Base Ball Players wasn't an organization of baseball clubs vying for a pennant as would be suspected. Actually, the NA was exactly what its title said it was — an association of *players* — and then some because it permitted anyone — including sportswriters — to belong to it. It had no union dues for the players or the clubs except the $10 a year each club had to pay to contend for the whip-pennant. When a convention was held, anyone could *attend and vote* on matters presented to the assemblage. In practice, each club sent a few delegates to confer with fellow baseball enthusiasts and make sure its interests were protected.

Henry Chadwick liked the NA because it let him take part in the decision-making process. The self-styled

"Father of the Game" was shocked by Hulbert's actions, especially because he wasn't consulted on the matter of forming a league of clubs. Hulbert chose not to ask his advice on the matter and continued to ignore him after the league was formed because Chadwick was considered by many Westerners to be a *butt-in-ski* and a blabbermouth through his newspaper columns.

Chadwick tried to be conciliatory in the beginning, actually almost taking credit for the founding of the league by suggesting that he had been the first to say the previous November that something had to be done about the gambling and drinking of the players and the duplicity of certain clubs' managers; but when Lewis Meacham in the Chicago *Tribune* and several other western newspaper writers, including the legendary Oliver Perry Caylor of the Cincinnati *Enquirer*, chided him for this stance, Chadwick became negative and accusatorial, charging the NL founders with acting illegally by ignoring the authority of the NA. Such nonsense was hardly worth rebutting by his colleagues across the nation, especially when the Association held it scheduled convention on March 1, 1876.

The remnants of the NA looked more like the *Pennsylvania association of professional base ball players* than any nationwide organization. Besides the Pennsylvanians, a few representatives from Ohio and Maryland attended. They were so few that instantly the delegates realized they were fighting a lost cause. They adjourned almost immediately, agreeing to meet again in Philadelphia the first part of April. That meeting turned out to be just as futile as the first, and Henry Chadwick's little group faded into the pages of history.

In the meantime, Al Spalding was putting the finishing

touches to his ball team. Although he had signed a contract with the Chicago club the previous year, Adrian Anson wanted to remain in Philadelphia with the Athletics. He had three reasons for his change of heart. The first was obvious: more money; and the second was the change in management by the Athletics: Spering's gang was out, and George Thompson was in. The third reason? Love. Anson's roots had begun to take hold in the Quaker City; to play in Chicago would mean leaving his girlfriend, Virginia Fiegel, behind. To show Hulbert and Spalding how serious he was about returning to Philadelphia, Anson signed a two–year contract with the Athletics for 1877–78. The Chicago magnates were unmoved; he had put his signature on their paper and they meant to hold him to it. But when the players began spring workouts at a local gymnasium, Anson wasn't among their number. March turned into April, and Spalding moved the team outdoors to train. Still no Anson.

At this same time, William J. Boyd of the Mutuals was having the same difficulty as Anson but with the New York club. Boyd wanted to return to Hartford where he had played in 1874. William Cammeyer of the Mutuals was just as adamant about Boyd as Hulbert and Spalding were about Anson.

Hulbert thought of giving Anson an ultimatum to either show up or risk being barred from the League forever, but Spalding prevailed upon the club president to give Anson a little more time. Adrian Anson was an honest man, and he would live up to his word. Spalding proved to be right. By the middle of the month, Anson joined his new teammates for practice sessions — right after the Mutuals expelled Boyd from the League for the season.

With every man in camp now, the White Stockings were set to take on all challengers. Hulbert even splurged on new uniforms which were navy blue trimmed with white, including a big white "C" for Chicago over the left chest, white stockings (of course), and caps in a rainbow of colors. Spalding came up with the idea of putting a differently colored hat on each player so the fans could distinguish them from afar. Surprisingly, the notion caught on with other teams.* Of course, the use of uniform numbers would have been simpler, but it must be remembered that the men of this age were still playing without gloves (except for some catchers). How could they be expected to think about player identification when they couldn't even figure out how to keep from suffering the intense pain of catching a hard baseball bare–handed?

Chicago had a solid lineup from top to bottom, starting with Captain Spalding. With the Red Stockings over the previous five years, he had won 207 games on the mound and had hit a steady .320, but he wasn't considered to be the best pitcher in the business, not with all those other stars playing behind him. Spalding's 57–5 record in '75 was written off as the result of solid teamwork.

Gradually, baseball was becoming a science of sorts and was gaining students yearly. It was in the mid–1870s that the idea of a regular catcher had some effect on how a pitcher performed. Spalding was one of the first to recognize this fact, so he talked his Boston batterymate, James Laurie "Deacon" White, into joining him in Chicago. This was the same Deacon White who had pulled the revolving trick in 1870 when he left Cleveland for

* In later years, Spalding carried the idea further by giving each player a differently colored shirt as well.

Chicago and returned before catching a single pitch for the White Stockings. When the Forest Citys called it quits in 1873, White was signed by Harry Wright to play in Beantown where he hit .382 that year, .321 in '74, and .355 in '75.

Cal McVey was the third of the so-called "Big Four" to leave the Red Stockings for the Windy City. Born and raised in Iowa, he started his pro career with the Rockford Forest Citys, then followed Spalding to Boston in 1871. He went his own way for one season, playing for the Lord Baltimore Club in '73, then rejoined the Red Stockings for the following season. He started out as a catcher but became a firstbaseman and a change pitcher in '75. In five NA seasons, he hit .362 overall and led the National Association in hits and runs scored in '74.

The final Boston *deserter* was second–sacker Roscoe Conkling Barnes, a 25–year–old native of Mt. Morris, New York. Under playing rules through 1876, a hit ball that landed in fair ground then went foul before passing either first or third base was called a "fair–foul" and was treated as a fair ball. Anyone who has ever laid down a bunt knows that it doesn't take much to get a little english on the ball off the bat. With some practice, a hitter could perfect the technique of dropping one down the line and having it spin off into foul ground, forcing the thirdbaseman to make a long run to retrieve it and making it practically impossible for him to throw out the runner. Ross Barnes made an NA career out of this method of reaching base safely. In fact, he was so good at it that he led the National Association in hitting twice (.402 in '73 and .372 in '75) and in hits and runs scored thrice ('71, '73, and '75).

Johnny Peters was one of those American success stories. Jimmy Wood noticed him when the White

Stockings played in St. Louis during the spring of 1870, and when Wood needed infield help later in the season, he gave Peters a shot. Johnny wasn't yet up to snuff as a pro, so he went to Canada to play for three seasons. When Wood was putting the 1874 Chicago nine together, he sent for Peters again. The kid still had good hands and a strong arm, but his hitting was a little weak yet — weak for the 1870s' liberal scoring rules — as he only averaged .278 and .277 in '74 and '75 respectively. Even so, Spalding kept the Missouri native on the White Stockings for '76 because the Chicago captain knew then that a shortstop's defensive play can make up a lot for any lack of offense.

Ezra Sutton was supposed to come with Adrian Anson to the White Stockings for '76, but he went back on his word and stayed in Philadelphia. That was just one more reason for Hulbert and Spalding to be so adamant about Anson holding up his end of the bargain they had struck.

Born and raised in Marshalltown, Iowa on April 17, 1851, Adrian Constantine Anson began his professional career with the same club as Spalding and McVey, the Rockford Forest Citys, after first helping to start a baseball program at Notre Dame University in South Bend, Indiana. His collegiate career lasted only one season. He hit .352 in his only campaign with Rockford, then moved to the Athletics for the next four seasons. After building a .381 average in '72, he *fell off* to .353 in '73, .367 in '74, and .318 in '75 (the year he began dating Miss Fiegel seriously). His low water mark in the final year of the NA was written off to discouragement. When a few of his teammates were caught throwing games, Anse merely went through the motions the rest of the year, resulting in a lower batting average.

In their first season in Chicago after playing in

Washington, Paul Hines and John Glenn had mediocre campaigns at the plate, hitting .276 and .261 respectively. Hines improved his mark to .314 in '75, but Glenn fell off to .234. But it wasn't their bats that kept them playing in Chicago in '76. Spalding needed swift outfielders, and few men covered the wide open spaces better than Hines and Glenn.

The third member of the starting pickets was Bob Addy, another man who started his pro career in Rockford. After playing for a non–National Association team in '72, he split the '73 season between the Red Stockings and the Philadelphia White Stockings. Then he played for Hartford in '74 and was back with Philadelphia in '75. Addy wasn't much of a hitter, only breaking the .300 level while playing for Boston. It was his defense that attracted Spalding to him. Addy's nickname was "The Magnet".

Rounding out the squad were Oscar Bielaski, Fred Cone, and Fred Andrus. All three were primarily outfielders. Bielaski was the only one with any real professional experience, having played two years for the Washington Nationals and one each with the Lord Baltimores and Chicago White Stockings. Cone played for Harry Wright at Boston. Andrus was a rookie. Seeing that the Chicago club of 12 men was too large and had to be reduced, Cone simply left the team early on and went to work at the Matteson House as a bartender, winding up his baseball playing career. Before the season was out, he started a new career as an umpire.

The NL had no set schedule other than the clubs agreed that for the first four weeks the four eastern teams would play among themselves and the four western nines would do likewise. Then the Westerners would head east for a complete round of games in each city, taking a week for travel which allowed them to play exhibition games along the way; and the Easterners would return the favor after that. At that point, the season would be half over, and they would repeat the same basic schedule.

The White Stockings were the odds on favorites at the beginning of the campaign, but Hartford and Boston were considered to be more than fair competition. The other five teams were rather unknown commodities, and no one was certain as to what they could or would do during the campaign.

1876 was the Centennial for the United States, so it was only appropriate that Boston and the Athletics had the honor of opening the National League's inaugural season in Philadelphia on Saturday, April 22. The Red Stockings were the winners of that first game, 6–5.

Chicago opened in Louisville on Tuesday, April 25. Henry Chadwick had predicted a few months earlier that 10,000 or more would turn out for the contest. Attendance was less than half that as Spalding pitched a seven-hit shutout and led the Whites in hitting with a 3–for–5 performance as Chicago won its first NL game, 4–0. Two days later he shut out Louisville again, 10–0. Spalding didn't just pitch the first shutout in National League history; he pitched the first *two* shutouts. The White Stockings swept a pair from the Reds in Cincinnati the next week. The second game of the series was marked by the first ever NL home run, an inside–the–park round–tripper hit by Ross Barnes.

From Porkopolis, the Whites traveled to St. Louis to meet the Browns. The River City newspapers were filled with stories about the invaders from the Lake City, and there was much bragging about which was the better team, the Browns or the Whites. The first game of the two–game set was postponed due to wet grounds and was reslated for the following Monday. The second scheduled date met with no interference from the weather.

Chicago's first NL win had been a whitewash, so maybe it was appropriate that the White Stockings' first NL loss was also by goose eggs. Spalding ran up against curveballing George Washington Bradley who had been tough on the Whites the previous season. Bradley treated them no better in '76 as he threw a two–hitter and nipped Chicago on an unearned run, 1–0. The whitewash prompted one St. Louis scribe to pen a little ditty for his readers:

> *There's a town in the North called She–cag–o,*
> *Which is known far and wide for her brag–o.*
> *She sent her Whites down*
> *To sink the brave Browns*
> *But only ran foul of a snag–o.*

After two weeks of the season, Chicago was tied for first place with Hartford, both teams possessing 4–1 records. Boston, Cincinnati, and Philadelphia were a game and a half back each with 3–3 marks. St. Louis was in sixth, 2–3; Louisville seventh, 2–4; and New York last, 2–5.

Spalding and the White Stockings turned the tables on the Browns in their makeup game, winning, 3–2; then they headed for Chicago to open their first National League home stand.

Large crowds seemed to bring out the best in Al Spalding. Just as he had in the opener in Louisville, he shut out the Reds, 6–0, to begin the White Stockings' Chicago campaign. The Whites went on to win four more games on that stand, losing only to George Bradley when St. Louis came to town.

When the Westerners headed east to visit the other half of the League, the White Stockings and Hartford were in a virtual tie for first place with 10–2 and 9–1 records, respectively, but Hartford was on top by percentage. St. Louis trailed both of them by three games, and Boston was four behind. The Athletics, Louisville, New York, and Cincinnati were in the second division, and all but the Mutuals were doomed to remain there throughout the rest of the season.

Chicago's first stop on their eastern swing was Hartford. The White Stockings won the first game of the three–game set and took possession of first place for a couple of days. Hartford came back to win the second contest, and there was talk that the mighty White Stockings weren't so mighty after all. Even so, when the Whites left town, they were back on top after winning the third game and would stay there for the next five weeks.

Boston was prepared for Chicago coming for Memorial Day. Seats for more than 500 additional spectators were erected, and all of the previously built stands were checked by the building inspectors to make certain they were safe for the expected huge throngs that would be sitting in them. Long before 2:00 p.m. every reserved seat was taken. The horse cars were full of passengers headed for the park where the gateways were already choked with throngs of clamoring customers. The people couldn't push and shove their way into the grounds fast enough. The only thing that kept the enclosure from being packed completely full — playing field and all — was the cessation of ticket sales. There were no tickets sold for one hour before the game started at 3:30. Yet so great was the rush of humanity that hundreds of anxious fans unable to buy ducats were pushed through the gates by the those who did. Many more devotees of the game climbed the fence and readily paid for so doing, glad to get in at any price. Inside the grounds the sight was indeed a remarkable one. A densely packed sea of heads lined each side of the playing field. The low seats in front were filled, and in front of these, fans were seated three and four rows deep. Each telegraph pole was a perch for two or three ad— mirers of the national game; every foot of room atop the lower fence was covered; and a thousand were seated on the grass below the centerfield fence. People kept com— ing in, overflowing onto the field and wandering about looking for places to sit or stand; and yet in the last half hour before the game, before the grounds were at last cleared and the game begun, the number of spectators didn't seem to increase perceptibly. While the players tried to warm up, the crowd toed the baselines and throwing was soon stopped as it was seen that the game couldn't start until the crowd was pushed back. 69 policemen, players of both sides, and officers of the Boston club worked for 20 minutes to get the crowd back; a long tedious process. To get them "outside" — off the playing field completely — was impossible as there wasn't room enough, but they were finally placed in bounds enough for play to start.

The people were remarkably impartial and good— natured. The crowd estimate was 12,000, including those who made their way in without paying. Receipts were $5,050, which meant 10,100 people paid to get in. Not a bad day in the counting room for the Boston club, but it was a bad day on the field for the Red Stockings. Spalding bested Joe Borden, 5–1.

The White Stockings reeled off six more wins on the

road before the Mutuals took them into camp in the next to last game of the tour. After winning the final contest in New York, Chicago had a 20–4 record but only a one-game lead over Hartford at 18–4. St. Louis was now a distant third at 14–10. The Mutuals, making their final first division appearance for '76 were in fourth at 10–13.

Then it was time for the eastern clubs to play in the West. On June 20, the largest number of ballplayers ever carried on one train — all eight NL clubs, 122 people in all, including umpires, officials, etc. — took the celebrated day train from Philadelphia over the Pennsylvania Railroad by daylight so as to get a good view of the Alleghenies and reach Cincinnati in the morning. There were 11 cars in all, including four Pullmans for the exclusive use of the ballplayers.

Back in Chicago again, the White Stockings swept the Mutuals during the first week, then took 2-of-3 from the Athletics the second.

The calendar read July 4; the United States of America was 100 years old. All across the nation Centennial celebrations were set to go. In Chicago, a whole day was planned for the city to salute the birth of the country, and it would end with an enormous fireworks display along the lakefront that night. But first there would be some fireworks at 23rd and State streets in the afternoon because the Hartford club was in town to face the White Stockings, who led the Easterners by a mere game and a half. Tommy Bond took the mound for Hartford and masterfully shut down the powerful hitting attack of his hosts, beating the White Stockings, 3–0. Hartford turned the trick again two days later, and suddenly, Chicago was in second place by a half game and — more importantly — by two losses. The Whites found their hitting clothes for the final game of the series but remained in second place for a few more days.

The National League standings of July 9 had Hartford in first, 24–6; Chicago second, 26–7; St. Louis third, 20–12; and Boston fourth, 17–16. No one else was even close to being in the pennant race.

Harry Wright's Boston Red Stockings were the last eastern team to visit Chicago in the first half of the season. The Bean Eaters were having trouble with their pitching, and it showed in the Windy City series. The White Stockings won all three games by scores of 18–7, 11–3, and 15–0. Chicago's sweep, coupled with three straight losses by Hartford to the Browns in St. Louis, put the White Stockings back in first place — for good as it turned out. The Whites went on to win their next seven contests to extend their winning streak to 11, their longest of the season.

During that run, Cal McVey had back–to–back 6–for–7 games, then Ross Barnes had a perfect 6–for–6 game one day later. By the end of July, Chicago was six and a half games up on Hartford and seven and a half on St. Louis. Cincinnati was eliminated by the Whites from the pennant race on July 29.

On the final Sunday of July, most of the sports print in the Chicago newspapers centered around the signing of players for the 1877 season. The *Tribune* had a most interesting quote that day, which seemed odd for that time as well as any future era when sportswriters took a harder line on club management:

> And this may be a good place to drop a para–
> graph in answer to several letters addressed
> to The Tribune asking why the Chicago Club

management don't engage their team for next year. *The answer is that Mr. Hulbert is doing just what is wisest under the circumstances* (author's italics); and, as he should be given the credit for assembling the only first–class team Chicago ever had, so he should be let alone in his movements for 1877. He will do just what is best, no doubt.

No doubt! The truth was Hulbert was deliberately waiting to sign players for '77. Although he had taken control of the team in '75 by buying some stock and demanding proxy powers from several stockholders, he didn't have majority ownership.

Hulbert knew that at any time things could go awry and the proxies he held could be withdrawn. To prevent this and to further consolidate his power, he tried to gain legal control of the club by buying up stock from his fellow owners. By the end of July, he had purchased 22 shares to add to his own single share, but he needed 13 more to gain control in his own name. When they weren't forthcoming, he conspired with the other officer of the club — the secretary, Albert Goodwill Spalding — to disenfranchise more than 20 stockholders by allowing the Chicago Base Ball Association to die an unethical — but very legal — death.

When the first charter from the state of Illinois was granted to the founders of the Chicago Base Ball Club in 1869, it was given a three–year time limit. When this charter expired in the fall of 1872, no one paid much attention to it because Chicago was too busy rebuilding from the catastrophic fire and the club had no team, only a playing facility. Finally, when plans were being made in '73 to field a new club for '74, a new three–year charter was obtained from the state. This charter came up for renewal in the middle of '76. If this wasn't done on time, then the Chicago Base Ball Association would cease to exist as a legal entity. It was this charter that Hulbert and Spalding let expire in the summer of '76.

At the same time, Hulbert, E.F. Dexter, and W.M. Murray then formed a new company named the Chicago Ball Club, incorporating it with $20,000 capital stock divided into 200 shares with a par value of $100 each. Hulbert made certain he was the majority stockholder. Murray and J. DeKoven subscribed liberally to the stock; Norman Gassette who had since seen the wisdom of Hulbert's ways, Dexter, and Bartlett took some shares each; Spalding, Ross Barnes, Cal McVey, and Deacon White also bought in; and the remaining shares were "snapped up by one of the largest capitalists in Chicago." This last was a ruse put in by the *Tribune* to give Hulbert's actions a tinge of legality.

This wasn't so bad — yet. Hulbert had done nothing wrong as far as the law was concerned until he commandeered the defunct corporation's biggest asset — the team. Hulbert and Spalding immediately signed up every man they wanted for the '77 squad, leaving the old club without players and with very little chance of obtaining a decent nine in time for the next year's campaign. When they did this, the two conspirators threw open the doors for a lawsuit by the disenfranchised stockholders whereby they could be charged with *deliberately* allowing the charter to expire in order to abscond with the corporation's property. As a possible way of heading off this trouble, Hulbert bought up the 13 additional shares he needed to gain legal control of the Chicago Base Ball Association from stockholders who saw the handwriting on the wall: Hulbert would have control and that was that! Hulbert then moved to dissolve the corporation — although it was already defunct — and hand over the assets to his new company, the Chicago Ball Club. This was a legal move but still very unethical. Not everyone was pleased.

The disenfranchised stockholders were furious, so they immediately began legal proceedings against Hulbert. The whole baseball community was aflutter with rumors about how it would turn out, but Hulbert wisely chose to avoid any court room battles by buying up the remaining shares of the deceased Chicago Base Ball Association — at inflated prices, of course, as part of the settlement. At long last, Hulbert had the club to run as he saw fit — and legally, too. He resumed the business of operating a baseball team in Chicago.

Although there had been a few rumors of gamblers sniffing around certain players in the League, none of the informal investigations conducted by the individual teams had turned up any evidence condemning anyone. In fact, just the opposite was true. Bobby Mathews, the New York pitcher who had been accused of throwing games the previous year, reported an attempt made by a gambler to bribe him into throwing a game. A little digging led the League sleuths from New York to Chicago and a whole ring of rigged pool sellers was uncovered. Nothing legal was done to these men, but the public exposure was enough to put them out of business, if not behind bars.

On August 3, 1876, the White Stockings were playing in Louisville when it started to rain. In those days, rain only stopped a game when the ball became too soggy for play. In the bottom of the fifth with the Whites at bat and leading by several runs and the rain coming down steadily, the Louisville nine made no effort to retire any Chicago hitters. It was easy enough for the umpire to see what Louisville was trying to do, so he ordered the Kentuckians to either begin playing in earnest or risk forfeiting the game. Jimmy Devlin's boys continued their charade on the next hitter, and the umpire made good on his threat, calling the game forfeit in favor of Chicago. Under 1876 rules, a game was still incomplete until both sides had finished hitting in the fifth inning. Under later rules, this would change; a game would be considered completed after four and a half innings if the home team was in the lead. This game with Louisville helped bring about this change. Good sport that he was, Spalding agreed to replay the game in its entirety, which Louisville won, although it made little difference in the outcome of the championship season.

By the middle of August, it was becoming evident that Philadelphia and New York were having some serious financial problems. Attendance was off in both cities. It was so bad in Philadelphia that for one game against Hartford the visitor's take of the gate receipts was only $3.75.

The White Stockings seemed to be coasting along through the season at this time. Then suddenly, the St. Louis Browns and George Washington Bradley jumped up, kicked them around a bit, and brought the Chicagoans back to reality. Bradley beat the Whites two straight in St. Louis, the second game being a one–hit shutout. But this wasn't the worst of it for Chicago. The third game of the series went into the bottom of the ninth with the White Stockings ahead, 6–5. With two out and St. Louis secondbaseman Mike McGeary on second, former Chicago player Scott Hastings bounced one down the line. Anson went to field it, but McGeary, coming down to third from second, stepped into Anse's way — some said he kicked the ball — interfering with the play. The ball rolled into foul ground past Anson, allowing Hastings to reach first safely and allowing McGeary to score. The umpire made no immediate decision, but the St. Louis fans did. They rushed en masse onto the field in celebration, thinking the Browns had won the game.

Spalding called on the umpire to call McGeary out for interference as the rules plainly stated that a runner couldn't interfere with the play of a fielder. The ump looked at the mob, called both men safe, and the score was tied. Spalding took his men from the field as a matter of discretion. Had he protested and the umpire decided in his favor, the fans might had gotten out of hand and someone could have been hurt. At least, he thought at the time that he and his mates were in a threatened position. The umpire then called the game a forfeit in St. Louis' favor, the first ever in the National League.

The next day in Chicago the Browns were in town for a rematch. It was no contest as the Whites pounded Bradley to the tune of 12-2. But that wasn't the message telegraphed to St. Louis that afternoon. Instead, the following went out:

> Office Chicago Courier, Chicago, Aug. 22 — The Browns driven from field: Bradley fatally injured; pressure too great for the Whites; 6 to 0 favor Browns; game decided in favor Browns, and in consequence umpire hung to one of the pillars of grand stand.

Bury My Heart at Wrigley Field

The hoax was accepted as reality in St. Louis for a few minutes until the real telegram came, announcing the real result. Even so, there were some who still believed the first report to be true, and they ran around the city trying to incite others to take up arms and head out for Chicago with blood in their eyes. Fortunately, nothing came of the joke except for St. Louis to get even at a later date.

The St. Louis set finished Chicago's season series with each of the western clubs. The White Stockings won 9-of-10 from Louisville, swept all 10 games from Cincinnati, but lost 6-of-10 to St. Louis. They had 16 games left to play with the eastern nines, and the first National League campaign would be history.

Chicago's magic number (any combination of Chicago wins and second place Hartford losses) for clinching the pennant was still at 14, and Hartford was only six games behind. Philadelphia, New York, and Louisville were eliminated with Cincinnati now. Boston's chances weren't good, and St. Louis wasn't in much better shape.

When the Whites arrived in Philadelphia for their first eastern set, they were greeted with the report that the Athletics had but $22 in their treasury and were on the verge of folding. Two sparse crowds for the Chicago games supported that rumor. The same circumstance was evident in New York, too; and if that wasn't enough to worry Hulbert, Tommy Bond quit the Hartford team, stating that Bob Ferguson, the team captain, was throwing games. Bond later withdrew the accusation, and Ferguson was exonerated. The White Stockings swept their four games that week, lowering their magic numbers over Hartford to 10, St. Louis to eight, and Boston to three.

Finally, on September 11, the expected happened. G.W. Thompson notified Hulbert that the Athletics would most likely be unable to complete their schedule of games to be played in the West and asked Hulbert if the Whites and Browns would consider playing the last series of games in Philadelphia instead, with both western clubs taking two–thirds of the gate receipts as if they were the home team. Thompson tempered his request with the excuse that the Centennial celebration shows were free.

Hulbert said no, sticking by and citing the rules that each team must complete its schedule or be expelled. His refusal made Philadelphia a dead club.

The next week the Mutes announced that they would be unable to make the last trip west to complete the season. Hulbert was angered by the problems in Philadelphia, but he was at least given warning of them. Not so with New York. Bill Cammeyer had told him on more than one occasion how the Mutuals were doing okay and would finish the season, and Hulbert repeatedly reassured the press that New York wouldn't fail. When Cammeyer couldn't keep his word, Hulbert was embarrassed and hurt. Cammeyer left Hulbert and the League directory no choice but to expel the Mutuals.

Two days later the White Stockings eliminated Boston from the race. St. Louis fell out of the race the following week, leaving only Hartford with any kind of chance of catching Chicago. All the Connecticut team had to do was win all 11 of its remaining games, including the final two games with the Whites in Chicago. Hartford gave it their best shot but couldn't win the first game from the Whites, and on September 26, 1876 the Chicago White Stockings clinched the first National League pennant.

9

Spalding Leaves The Field

The human body is so resilient in one instant and so fragile the next that a man can fall from a great height and not suffer anything worse than a bruise, then slip on a tiny patch of winter ice and break a leg in two places. Such is the caprice of life; a valuable lesson that Al Spalding learned in 1877.

The 1876 Chicago White Stockings had been just short of magnificent. As a team, they had won 52 of the 66 games they had played against league competition. Although they had led the loop throughout most of the campaign, they weren't the runaway champions that so many historians have said they were. If not for the personal differences between Bob Ferguson and Tommy Bond that split the Hartford club and unsettled the team, the Connecticut nine might have won the first NL flag.

Individually, the White Stockings were unequalled. Ross Barnes won the batting title, hitting a solid .429 under the rules of the day. Joining him among the league leaders were Adrian Anson at .356 in third, Johnny Peters at .351 in fourth, and Cal McVey at .347 in fifth. Deacon White (.343), Paul Hines (.331), Spalding (.312), and John Glenn (.304) also had excellent seasons at the bat. Only Oscar Bielaski and Bob Addy failed to hit .300.

White led the league in RBIs with 60, and he was followed in the NL lists by four teammates: Hines, Barnes, and Anson with 59 each, and McVey with 53. Barnes topped the league in hits with 138, and Peters and Anson were second and third with 111 and 110 respectively. Barnes also finished first in runs scored with 126, walks with 20, slugging percentage at .590, total bases with 190, and triples with 14. He only shared the doubles title with Hines and Dick Higham of Hartford with 21 each.

Spalding won 47 games to top the league, but a lot of his victories were due to his supporting cast's potent offense and superb fielding. Barnes, Peters, and Hines were the best fielders in the league at their respective positions, and overall, Chicago was second to St. Louis at handling the ball.

But not all was rosy in '76. At least not for all of professional baseball.

With the formation of the National League, the National Association bit the dust in reality, although it tried to survive on paper. Several cities claimed to have professional nines, but most were actually semi-pro clubs with only a few players being salaried. These teams competed for the sake of sport and making money, much the same as the organized clubs did before the formation of the pro association in '71; they weren't playing for any sort of a championship other than a mythical title made up by local sportswriters.

The National League also had its problems. New York and Philadelphia failed to complete their respective schedules, both clubs folding near the end of the season. And there were the constant rumors of gambling by various players who were throwing games for "pool-rings" in Chicago, Philadelphia, and New York. At the League meeting in December 1876 at Cleveland, the

153

first order of business was the expulsion of the Athletics and Mutuals from the NL. Bill Cammeyer of New York accepted his club's fate and didn't even bother to attend the confab. George Thompson of Philadelphia recognized the benefits of belonging to the pro circuit and was present at the conference, even presenting a letter pleading for mercy. It was all for naught as Chicago president Bill Hulbert led the four western clubs in a movement to remove the two eastern clubs from the organization. By a unanimous vote, the Mutuals and Athletics were given the boot. Of course, everyone besides the league magnates thought this was only a temporary move, that come spring both teams would be permitted to rejoin the circuit. Everyone but the owners was wrong.

There followed a very important amendment to the League's constitution that has carried through time in spirit if not in word. The League authorities put into place a statute that forbade them from tampering with players on teams outside the League, providing that those teams signed an agreement to do likewise and then paid the NL $10 for such protection. The teams that entered into this arrangement with the NL became part of a quasi-official organization known as the League Alliance. A full 13 clubs joined the LA and began play for their own championship that spring. The National League teams scheduled several exhibitions with these teams, too.

The next item on the agenda was changing some playing rules.

One had a severe effect on the White Stockings' Ross Barnes, the man who had made a science of hitting the ball close to the foul lines, having it land fair then go foul before passing first or third base. This was a fair ball until '77. Beginning with that year, the rule was changed to state that the ball had to remain in fair territory until passing either first or third base in order to be a fair hit. This move ruined Barnes' batting average in future years.

Other changes included enlarging the bases to 15 inches on a side; moving home base — which was the same size and shape as the other three bases — into fair ground; restricting baserunners to stay within the base-paths; and forbidding batters to interfere with catchers when they were trying to throw out a runner or field a throw from a baseman. The final and maybe the most significant rule change was the one where the coin toss was done away with and the home team was required to bat first in every game. The thinking behind this was it would make the game a little more even if the visitor had the last turn at bat on their opponent's field.

The magnates were in a penny-pinching mood, too. The owners decided to pay the players only 50 cents per diem for meals, and they would henceforth charge them $30 a season for uniforms and for repairing and washing same. Catchers would be charged for each "pair" of gloves they wore.*

The last important consideration for the League of-ficials was the election of a new president to succeed Morgan Bulkeley. The high society banker was stepping down, ostensibly to enter politics.** In years to come, he

---

* A "pair" consisted of a catching glove and a throwing glove that had the fingers cut off.

** The true motive for Bulkeley leaving the club is a debatable point when the fact that the Hartford club was in deep financial trouble is considered. Hartford

would be Hartford's mayor, Connecticut's governor, and a U.S. Senator from that state.

Hulbert nominated Nick Apollonio of Boston to head up the league, but Apollonio declined to serve on the basis that he didn't expect to be with the Red Stockings in the future. The magnates then turned to the man who had begun the whole affair in the first place, the man they had wanted to be president the previous winter when they established the National League in New York; and Bill Hulbert was elected unanimously. With that the convention adjourned.

Now that Hulbert was in charge of the entire League, he had less time to run his own club. So he turned over the reins of power, although not the accompanying title, to Spalding, the Chicago Ball Club's secretary, manager, and field captain.

Spalding relished the challenge. Already he had won a pennant and had helped Hulbert turn a profit for the club in its first NL season. Now it was his turn to prove he could do it without Hulbert.

One of the benefits of expelling the Mutuals and Athletics from the League was the nullification of any player contracts those clubs had. Both Adrian Anson and George Bradley had signed to play for Philadelphia in '77, but when the A's were given the heave-ho, they were free to sign with any other team. Spalding wasted no time in getting their signatures on Chicago contracts.

was in such bad shape that the stockholders voted to play their 1877 home games in Brooklyn at Union Grounds where the Mutuals had played in previous years. The team was known as the Hartford Brooklyns or the Brooklyn Hartfords throughout the '77 season.

Of course, the eastern press screamed that this was Hulbert's design in the first place when he — as if Hulbert had acted alone — expelled New York and Philadelphia. Spalding went to spring training with a sore arm and a full roster that included returnees Anson, Barnes, Peters, Hines Glenn, and McVey and new—comers Charlie Waitt and George Washington "Grin" Bradley, the same Bradley who had been the Whites number one mound nemesis in '75 and '76. It was Spalding's theory that the curveballing Bradley and he would make a fine pair or moundsmen in that Grin was tough on certain teams and he was hard on the others; together, they would make Chicago reign supreme again.

Such wasn't the case, however.

Almost from its very start, the baseball season of '77 seemed to go wrong. The Cincinnati club was expelled after playing only five games because its management failed to pay League dues, and the remaining League clubs were finding it difficult to schedule each other, often playing League Alliance teams in their own areas instead of traveling to the other section of the country to play NL opponents. Milwaukee, Indianapolis, Syracuse, and Pittsburgh had strong LA nines, and there were the usual pro teams in several large towns throughout the East.

As far as League play was concerned, by the first of July, Boston and Hartford were well ahead of the pack at 12–6 and 11–7 respectively. Louisville and St. Louis were tied for third at 8–10, the White Stockings were 7–12, and reorganizing Cincinnati was 2–3.

Only weeks before, the National League appeared doomed to failure, but with the resumption of play by the Cincinnati Reds under new management there was hope again that the only real all pro circuit would succeed.

Things were looking so bright that the sportswriters of the day found time to inject a little humor into their pages on occasion. An unknown scribe at the Syracuse *Courier* took time out to find out who really was the father of the curveball.

> Tommy Bond has put forth a doubtful claim to the invention of the parabolic–curve pitching. For is there not in Holy Writ a statement that when Noah was building the ark he "pitched it within and without?" What more does any curve pitcher do?

Then things went bad again, and the situation in the National League in early August appeared to be total confusion. No one really seemed to know if the Cincinnati club was in the NL or not. The newspapers were running two sets of standings; one that included Cincinnati and counted all its games, and a second that excluded the Reds completely. There were arguments pro and con about allowing the Reds to participate in the championship season, but nothing was final until the League meeting that winter.

As for play on the field, Harry Wright proved himself as the best captain (field manager of his day as he led the Red Stockings to the '77 pennant, using a well trained, well conditioned team of regulars, seven of them having played for Boston in '76. Wright knew the secret to success: continuity, clubs that employed the same men year to year were usually winners. Every other team in the League shuffled men in and out of their lineups, and this proved to be their downfall. A lot of this was caused by injuries and illnesses, often to key players; but mostly it was a matter of money: instead of giving a guy a well earned raise, a team would let him go in favor of a less talented man who would play for fewer bucks.

Before the season began, Chicago was the favorite to win the pennant, but almost immediately, Ross Barnes came down with a serious illness and couldn't play effectively. Then Spalding was lost as a pitcher, moving to first base where he wore a pair of the gloves his firm manufactured. George Bradley couldn't make the new, harder ball curve as well as the softer ball used by the League the previous year. Cal McVey proved his best position was first base, not catcher. Not only did the team's fielding and pitching fall apart, so did its hitting. Only McVey hit better in '77 (.368) than he had in '76 (.347.) Adrian Anson and Johnny Peters were the only other regulars to hit over .300 at .337 and .317 respectively.

At season's end, many newspapers around the country were celebrating the final campaign of the National League. Henry Chadwick was particularly joyful in print. No longer would the western clubs dominate the game; the power would return to his beloved New York. Or so he thought.

In reality, the National League had suffered serious heart palpitations but was resting quietly in the off season when the directors of the Louisville club decided it was time to question their players about the gambling rumors that had been flying around them for weeks. On October 26 and 27, they called Bill Craver, George Hall, Jimmy Devlin, Al Nichols, George Shaffer, Joe Gerhardt, George Latham, Bill Crowley, Charles "Pop" Snyder, and Bill Hague to testify. Almost from the start of the hearings, Hall and Devlin couldn't keep quiet about their gambling activities, each pointing the finger at the other as to which one enticed the other to cross the line into criminal territory. By the time it was all over, Hall, Devlin, Nichols, and Craver* were all banished from the NL forever, and the eastern scribes chuckled with delight as they tried to drive a poison pen into the heart of the National League.

The League meeting was held December 4–6, 1877 at the Kennard House in Cleveland. The Hartford club had disbanded, and St. Louis surprised everyone by resigning from the League. This left the National League with only three official members: Chicago, Boston, and Louisville. The board of directors acted immediately on the matter of which set of standings to accept for the past season: the one with Cincinnati's games included or the one without the Reds. Unanimously, they chose to exclude Cincinnati, making the Chicago White Stockings the first team in NL history to go from the penthouse to the cellar in one season.

Then the board upheld the expulsion of the four Louisville players. With that piece of distasteful business out of the way, they acted on the applications for admission to the League.

Cincinnati, Milwaukee, and Indianapolis asked to join the circuit, and a new Hartford group pushed to be recognized as a League member. Cincinnati's rejoining was a foregone conclusion because of a prior deal made between the club and Hulbert during the '77 season in

* Craver's banishment was due to insubordination when he refused to permit the club's officials to examine his telegrams. When they did it anyway, they discovered that he was innocent of the gambling charge. Even so, they upheld the expulsion because he was a troublemaker.

which he promised to readmit the Reds if they would play out the schedule, which they did. Indianapolis was admitted because it had the best record of all the teams in the League Alliance, and Milwaukee was brought in because it allegedly had a solid organization. The Hartford group wasn't recognized as a member because that franchise had belonged to Bob Ferguson and he had thrown in the towel and had accepted employment with the Chicago White Stockings as captain for '78, thus terminating Hartford's membership in the NL. The new Hartford contingent had tried to assume ownership of a franchise that no longer existed, but Hulbert refused to allow this to happen.

The board then passed a resolution that expressly forbade the playing of games on Sundays. All that remained to do was the changing of a few minor playing and scoring rules, rewrite the formats for choosing umpires, and enter into a business arrangement similar to the one employed for the '77 season. Then the magnates adjourned until the following year.

Over the winter, Louisville withdrew from the NL and the Hartford group that claimed the bones of Morgan Bulkeley's deceased Hartford Base Ball Club was admitted as the Providence Baseball Association. This kept the League at six teams for the '78 season.

Gradually, professional baseball was moving toward total organization. The National League was the oldest circuit and had six teams in competition for its pennant. The year before the International Association was formed by seven teams from Canada and upper New York state, and the League Alliance was brought into existence by Hulbert and the directors of the NL. On the West Coast, a professional league came springing to life during the winter and took the name of Pacific Coast League. Some pro teams in smaller cities remained independent, but their life expectancy was short.

In Chicago, Al Spalding was lamenting over what he had or hadn't done for the White Stockings in '77. According to Henry Chadwick, the fall of the Chicago club in the standings was due to bad management, meaning Spalding had done a spurious job of it because he "had too many irons in the fire." This was only partially true.

The Whites had won it all in '76 because they had the best talent in the League and the players stayed healthy; it would have been nearly impossible for that group of athletes not to win the pennant. In other words, Spalding didn't have to do much managing at all. The same wasn't true in '77. As a field leader, his mediocrity displayed itself glaringly when he failed to get his team to overcome the least bit of adversity.

However, Chadwick was correct about Spalding having spread himself too thin to handle his responsibilities properly.

Spalding and his brother Walter drew up a partnership agreement in February 1876 that put them in the sporting goods business together. They opened their store at 118 Randolph Street in the Loop the following month using $800 of their mother's money as their initial capital. It was Spalding's intent that Walter run the business while he provided publicity by playing baseball for the White Stockings. This was all well and good, but it didn't quite work that way. Spalding had to spend more time at the store than he had planned because he was too good at bringing in business to be done on credit which restricted the company cashflow and made hiring workers prohibitive. A.G. Spalding and Bro. was so busy that Spalding's mother and sister had to pitch in and help by doing much of the sewing of the custom-made uniforms the firm sold.

Spalding's club workload grew in '77 when Hulbert practically turned over the presidential reins of the White Stockings to him because Hulbert was too busy overseeing the entire National League. The manufacturing part of Spalding's sporting goods business grew rapidly that year also, partly due to the work thrown to him by the NL when A.G. Spalding & Bro. was hired to publish the League book, which contained the rules and constitution and results of the previous year. Along with this, Spalding published Spalding's Official Baseball Guide, which he passed off as being officially sanctioned by the secretary of the National League, Nick Young.

Realizing his managerial and business duties were too important to his future as a player and captain of the White Stockings, Spalding wisely hired a new leader for the Chicago club for '78.

Robert Ferguson was already well traveled in professional baseball when he accepted the job as captain of the White Stockings for '78. He had played for and captained the New York Mutuals, Brooklyn Atlantics, and Hartford before coming to Chicago; and he had served as president of the old National Association for three years. Somewhere along the line he had been given the most unusual nickname in the annals of all sports when someone dubbed him "Death to Flying Things". Born in Brooklyn in 1845, he was on the down side of his playing career at 32. Always an infielder, he slated himself to fill the shortstop position for the Whites in '78.

Ferguson wasn't the only player to leave the defunct

Hartford club for greener pastures. He brought four others with him: Joe "Old Reliable" Start, John Cassidy, Bill Harbidge, and Frank "Terry" Larkin. All through the previous summer and fall, rumors were rampant about where the "Hartford gang" was headed. Some newspapers had them going to Philadelphia to revitalize the Athletic Club. Another had them going to Troy; a third staying in Brooklyn where they would form a new Atlantic Club. When they wound up in Chicago, every-one felt certain the Whites would be back in the pennant race in '78.

Joe Start was an oldtimer as far as ballplayers went in those days, being born in New York City in 1842. In five years in the old National Association, all with the New York Mutuals, he compiled a .282 batting average, and he hit .277 for New York in the National League in '76 and .332 for Hartford in '77. He was a sure-handed first-sacker who led the League in fielding his position in '76.

Like Ferguson, Johnny Cassidy hailed from Brooklyn. He started his pro career in New Haven in '75, then moved to the Brooklyn Atlantics in mid-season. He hit a weak .162 for the year. He was playing semi-pro ball when Ferguson suddenly needed a spare outfielder late in the '76 season, bringing him to Hartford. Cassidy hit .277 in 12 games, so Ferguson gave him another shot in '77. The Irishman responded by hitting .378.

Bill Harbidge was born in Philadelphia in 1855. He began his pro career with Hartford in '75 as a substitute, hitting a meager .216. He didn't get much better over the next two years, only moving up to .217 and .222 in '77. He did find a regular position as a catcher after under-studying the great backstopper of the era, Doug Allison, for three seasons.

Terry Larkin pitched only one game for the Mutuals in '76, then was the regular starter for Hartford in '77, winning 29 games and losing 25. His 501 innings pitched didn't top the League, but they did prove that he had the stamina to be a steady hurler.

Other newcomers to the White Stockings included Jack Remsen, Frank Hankinson, and Bill McClellan. The only players returning from the previous season were regular Adrian Anson, substitute Jimmy Hallinan, and change pitcher Laurie Reis who joined the Whites late the year before.

Remsen began his pro career in his home town with the Brooklyn Atlantics in '72, then joined the Mutuals in '74. He moved on to Hartford in '75, then jumped to the St. Louis Browns in '77. His four–year average in the NA was .247, then he hit .275 in '76 and .260 in '77.

New York–born Hankinson and Chicago native McClellan were both rookies.

Besides a nearly all new team, the White Stockings were given a new playing field. Lake Front Park was built on the same site as its namesake that was destroyed in *The Great Chicago Fire*. The layout of the diamond and the seating arrangements were different from the former park in that it was a "fer piece to left and just a healthy spit with the wind to right." The right field fence was so close that a ball hit over it was considered a ground rule double instead of a home run.

A month before the opening of the regular season the League magnates met in Buffalo for the purpose of drawing up a schedule for the coming campaign. At the same time, they were joined by representatives of the International Association clubs. The two organizations agreed in writing to permit games between the teams of their circuits to be played after the conclusion of the NL championship season in September.

The White Stockings got the season off to a decent start, winning their first three games in Indianapolis before losing three straight in Cincinnati. After two weeks of competition, the Whites trailed the Reds by three full games, and Cincinnati led the League with a perfect 6–0 mark.

On the first Sunday in June, Cincinnati had slowed down a bit, having an 11–4 record and a two and a half–game lead over Boston at 6–4. The Whites had fallen on hard times and stood at 5–9 and five and a half games back. Chicago's slow start was due to poor hitting. Ferguson led the team with a .314 mark, and Anson was next best with .276. After them, it was Harbidge and Larkin at .275, Start .259, McClellan .236, Cassidy .214, Remsen .164, and Hankinson .163. If not for Larkin's strong pitching, the Whites would have been in the cellar for sure.

By the end of June, Boston overtook Cincinnati and had a game and a half lead on the Reds. The White Stockings had moved up to third place with a 14–12 record and were only two and a half back. Indianapolis, Providence, and Milwaukee made up the second division. Two weeks later the Whites passed the Reds but trailed Boston by three and a half games.

On July 21, Chicago got as close to first place as they would for the remainder of the season when they pulled within one and half games of the Red Stockings. The White Stockings' record peaked at 26–15 on August 4, then disaster struck. In a showdown series with Boston the following week, the Whites lost four straight and found themselves six and a half games out.

Providence added two more losses to the streak, and

Cincinnati knocked White Stockings out of second place the week after that. On the last day of August, Boston pounded in the final nail, and the White Stockings were eliminated from the pennant race, finishing the season in fourth place at .500 with 30 wins and as many losses.

Former Chicago secondbaseman Ross Barnes added a little spice to the summer of '78 when he filed a lawsuit against the club for the wages he wasn't paid during his illness in '77; he asked for $1,000. The *Tribune* immediately sided with the Chicago club, but Spalding got the case put off until after the end of the playing season. The delaying tactic worked perfectly for Spalding and the club as Spalding could now cite precedents of other players not being paid when either injury or illness kept them from playing. Unfortunately for Barnes, these precendents were set during the '78 season, and the judge allowed them to be used by the defense. Barnes insinuated to the press that the judge was on *someone's payroll, but he still lost his case.*

The country wasn't in the best of financial conditions that year. A recession gripped the nation and the National League.

President Hulbert called an unprecedented summer meeting of owners in Providence on August 10. After conferring with his fellow magnates, he issued a statement on the economic conditions around the circuit and what the clubs intended to do about them.

For the most part, every team was losing money; Chicago and Boston were doing okay and Cincinnati was barely staying alive, but the other three clubs were losing dollars day in and day out.

Of course, the economy was partly to blame, but

Hulbert said the biggest cause of their monetary woes was the salary demands of the players. Therefore, a salary ceiling based on the previous year's ('78 income would be applied for the '79 season).

Also, there would be standardized contracts through-out the NL in '79, and these new agreements would run only from April 1 through September 30 of the year, thereby forcing the players not to rely totally on their baseball income for the entire year and encouraging them to seek off season employment.

These were monumental changes in the structure of player-owner relations, but few men of the time recognized them as such. Not until several years later did the players recognize what Hulbert and the other owners were doing to them, but by then it was too late to effectively fight back.

10

Anson Takes the Reins

1878 was the magical third year for baseball. This was the first season in which every single National League team that began the campaign in May finished it in September. Stability had seemingly come to the circuit, spreading out from Chicago.

As the '78 championship season wound down and it became apparent that Boston would win its second straight National League pennant, Al Spalding made the smartest management move of his career with the Chicago club. He signed Adrian Anson to a contract for the '79 campaign and made him captain of the team. From that time on, the Iowa native became known to his players as "Cap" (short for Captain) Anson.

Although Spalding had little trouble inking Anson to his fourth straight season in Chicago, the club's business manager and secretary did have his problems filling out the roster.

Prior to the end of the '78 season, the other teams had signed most of the loop's outstanding players for the following year — or so the rumors said until the League meeting in December.

Going into the confab held again in Cleveland, everyone knew that Milwaukee would be expelled for not paying its players and not paying some other bills.

Bury My Heart at Wrigley Field

President William Hulbert and the other owners wasted no time in removing the Cream City club from the League's roster. The next item on the agenda was to accept the Star Club of Syracuse, Bison Club of Buffalo, and the Cleveland Club of Cleveland into the circuit. Hulbert smiled broadly because his BABY now had a full complement of teams again. It was only momentary though because the Indianapolis club dropped a bombshell on the convention by resigning from the loop for financial reasons. Nonplussed, Hulbert rapped his gavel and said it was time to get on to other business: the rule changes.

Harry Wright had ceased to be much of an active player after the '74 National Association campaign. He did play in one game in each of the succeeding years, but his primary concern was directing his team on the field. In reality, Wright was the first dugout field manager in the history of the game when he stopped being the captain of the Boston Red Stockings in '78 and began running the team from the bench. He had done the same thing the year before, the year before that, and the year before that; except in previous campaigns, he had worn a Red Stockings uniform instead of street clothes.

For unexplained reasons, the other managers and captains in the League thought this gave the Red Stockings an unfair advantage during a game, so they passed a new rule that excluded all persons from the playing field except the players and the local police who were present to make certain the "lunatics" stayed in their seats and didn't interfere with the game. Of course, Wright protested but to no avail. Oddly, his own team's owner, Arthur Soden, voted with Hulbert and the others.

Playing rules that were changed or modified were:

Every "unfair ball" — a ball that was not a strike —

became a ball and eight balls resulted in the batter taking his base.

Intentionally hitting a batter with a pitch became a fineable offense where the umpire could assess the pitcher anything from $10 to $50.

In previous years, the man who made the last out in an inning was considered to be the last man to bat, whether he made the final out as a batter or a baserunner. The next man in the batting order would hit first in the fol-lowing inning, even if he had been at bat, had batted last, or had been on base during that frame. For example: Anson is on second, Start is on first, and Ferguson is at bat with two outs; Ferguson lines a single to left; but the leftfielder throws Anson out at the plate; Start would lead off the next inning because Anson had made the final out of that inning. For '79, the modern rule was established where the hitter after the last man to have an official plate appearance in an inning would lead off the next inning.

The last major rule change was the elimination of the one–hop out of a foul fly. No longer could a fielder catch a ball on the first hop in foul ground and the batter be called out. The fielder had to catch the ball on the fly to retire the hitter.

There was one special bit of business that Hulbert introduced to the convention. A resolution of respect to the memory of the late Lewis Meacham of the Chicago *Tribune* was passed honoring the sportswriter for his part in the formation of the National League. Meacham had died suddenly just weeks before the convention.

After a protracted and exciting discussion over the adoption of a uniform ball to be used by all of the clubs, the Spalding ball was adopted. The offer by Spalding to supply the balls without charge, an advertising idea, was the principle inducement.

With Milwaukee and Indianapolis now out of the League, the players those clubs had signed for '79 became free agents.

Spalding and Anson went over the list of men available to them and put together a solid nine for the coming year. For starters, Spalding was able to retain Bill Harbidge, Jack Remsen, Frank Hankinson, and Terry Larkin. From Milwaukee, they got Abner Frank Dalrymple and former White Stockings player Johnny Peters back for his third term in Chicago; and from Indianapolis, they picked up George "Orator" Shaffer, Joseph L. Quest, Edward Nagle "Ned" Williamson, and Frank Sylvester "Silver" Flint. To fill out the roster, Spalding came up with George Gore who had played with New Bedford in the International Association in '78.

As the regular catcher in '78, Harbidge hit .296 and had a fielding average of .878. Centerfielder Remsen hit only .232 but led the League in fielding his position at .944. Hankinson hit .267 and fielded .875 at third base. Larkin won 29 games and posted a 2.24 ERA, but he also lost 26 games; most of them in late season when his arm tired and the production behind him fell off. Peters had been one of the bright spots on the dismal Milwaukee nine, hitting .309 and fielding .853 as the regular second-baseman.

The big acquisitions for the White Stockings were Dalrymple and Shaffer for their offense and Williamson, Flint, Quest, and Gore for their defense.

Abner Dalrymple was a native of Warren, Illinois, born in 1857. He began his big league career the year before and hit a solid .354 for Milwaukee, which was the second best mark in the NL. He was no great shakes as an outfielder, so the Cream City captain put him in left field.

Anson penciled him in for the same position when he came to Chicago.

"Orator" was Philadelphia–born George Shaffer's nickname in baseball and with good reason: the man couldn't keep his mouth shut for more than half a minute. He began his NL career in '77 with Louisville and hit a reasonable .285 that year. When the Kentucky club folded, he went to Indianapolis where he rapped out hits at a .338 rate. As an outfielder, he was adequate.

Ned Williamson, born in Philadelphia in the same year as Dalrymple, was also an NL rookie in '78 after gaining pro experience with the Allegheny Club of Pittsburgh. He posted an unimpressive .232 batting average and fielded a fair .867 for Indianapolis. Anson saw potential in the young third–sacker, especially in Williamson's quickness afoot and rifle arm.

Joe Quest's anemic .205 wasn't why Anson wanted the diminutive infielder. It was his speed. Quest was base–ball's prototype secondbaseman for the next several generations. He stood 5'6" and weighed all of 150 pounds. Quest had 60 errors during his rookie season in Indianapolis, but this didn't mean that much in an era where almost every touched ball that wasn't fielded cleanly was called a muff. Anson noted that little Joe got a hand on grounders that most other men wouldn't even come close to. The miscues be hanged! He stopped more hits than he allowed baserunners via bobbles.

Frank Flint was the fourth second–year man Spalding picked up for Anson over the winter and the third who hailed from Philadelphia. Flint played for the Covington (Kentucky) Stars in '76 before joining the Indianapolis club in '77. He caught in 59 games for the Indiana entry to the League in '78, and his .908 average behind the plate was second best in the NL. He only hit .224, but

Anson didn't care about that. It was Flint's League-leading 102 assists that impressed the Chicago captain. Also, Flint played like Anson did: aggressively.

Rookie George Gore caught Anson's eye during an exhibition game the previous season against an upstate New York nine. He liked how the speedy outfielder covered his territory in center and asked Spalding to sign him for the White Stockings. Gore hit .324 in '78, but he achieved that average against mostly International Association competition while playing for New Bedford. George was the first native of Maine to play in the National League.

For the most part, Anson had an inexperienced bunch of ball players for the '79 campaign. He, Peters, Remsen, and Harbidge were the only ones who could trace their pro roots back to the days of the National Association. Larkin was entering his fourth season in the NL, and Shaffer was beginning his third. Five men were sophomores, and Gore was just starting out. The only real star among them was Anson himself, but he had never captained a team before, making him the biggest question mark of all.

While Anson was planning for the coming season, Hulbert was taking a postal poll of club owners on a new Troy club's application to join the League. There were no objections, and the National League once again had eight teams.

January '79 also marked the beginning of the first legitimate minor league in the country when teams from Peoria and Rockford, Illinois and Davenport and Dubuque, Iowa banded together to form the North-western League. The International Association and the National Alliance weren't real leagues in that they functioned in the same manner as the defunct National

Association had: with no set schedule or central authority.

Finally, April and the preseason rolled around. Anson satisfied himself with having his charges play amongst themselves and the best of the amateurs in the Chicago area. While practicing on the afternoon of April 15, the team captain was at bat and Terry Larkin was in the pitcher's box. Anson smacked a liner back through the box that caught Larkin totally unaware. Before he could react, the ball ricocheted off the side of his head, knocking him down and into a very groggy state. For the next few days, he was shaky on his feet but insisted that he was all right, which was good enough for Anson to keep him in uniform.

Spalding continued with his idea of identifying the players for the fans by giving each of them a differently colored cap, carrying it a little further in '79 by including a tie, belt, and stripe on the stocking, all matching the hat's color. Other than these colorful accessories, the uniform's pants, shirt, and socks were white. There was one little change in the attire that the newspapers pointed to with pride at times and with scorn and ridicule at others, depending on whether the club was winning or losing. Spalding added a touch of class when he had their hose made of silk. This led to the scribes calling them the Silk Stockings or Silks for the better part of the campaign.

Satisfied with Larkin's appraisal of his health, Anson put him in the pitcher's box for the opening game of the season against the Syracuse Stars. Larkin showed no ill effects from the collision of his head and the ball off Anson's bat, and Chicago trimmed the Stars, 4–3. Anson contributed a pair of singles and an RBI to his first managerial victory.

After their opening day victory, the White Stockings won five more before finally losing to Providence. Chicago started another streak that ran to 10 wins before Providence halted Anson's juggernaut again on June 6. By the end of the month, the Silks sat on top of the League standings with a 23–4 record, four full games ahead of Providence and nine ahead of Boston and Buffalo.

The only thing that slowed the team for just a moment was an incident in Indianapolis when the players were returning from a series in Cincinnati. Police boarded their train and made a serious search for Flint, Shaffer, and Quest, all three of whom had played for the Indianapolis nine the year before and who had left town without paying some of their bills. Flint and Shaffer hid in the baggage car, but Quest was caught and hauled off the train. Before the coppers could drag his secondbaseman too far, Anson paid little Joe's debt of $55 and got him back. The amazing thing was Shaffer being able to keep his mouth shut long enough for the officers to pass over him and Flint. It was clearly decided that the team would travel around Indianapolis in the future.

The most fateful day of '79 for the White Stockings came on August 4 in Dubuque, Iowa. Spalding accepted an invitation from a local promoter to bring the Chicago nine to the river city for an exhibition game on that Monday afternoon. They arrived in Dubuque the night before.

At the time, the Whites led the National League with a 35–12 mark. Providence was five and a half games back at 30–18; Buffalo six and a half back at 28–18; and Boston seven and a half out at 28–20. Anson was hitting a League leading .409. Ned Williamson was third at .354; Ab Dalrymple, .331 in eighth; and Shaffer, .326 in tenth.

The only bad moment was the release of Bill Harbidge for "bad habits". For all practical purposes, the race appeared to be over and the White Stockings would soon win their second title in four years.

Then it happened in Dubuque. Cap Anson ate something that didn't agree with him, and the next morning he complained of severe abdominal pains. A doctor diagnosed the trouble as a "liver disorder", a sort of 19th century catch-all term for any pain in the area of the stomach that was accompanied by jaundice.

Possibly, Anson had a case of hepatitis or a mild form of yellow fever. The latter was more the likely because of the accompanying stomach pains and nausea, both symptoms of the virus carried by some mosquitoes.

Whatever his illness, Anson sat out the exhibition, but Flint didn't. The gutsy catcher took a foul ball off his right hand and suffered two dislocated fingers.

Flint missed the next four games, and the Whites lost three of them. Anson missed six games, then bravely played one, going 1-for-4. That night he took to his bed again, sicker than ever. With Anson out of the lineup, Chicago gradually lost control of first place, losing the lead for the first time all season on August 18. "It looks like goodbye to the championship now," wrote a Chicago *Tribune* sportswriter. The Whites regained a share of the top spot five days later, tying Providence, both teams with 41-20 records. Hulbert told the *Tribune* : "I put some powder into the boys."

Not enough though because two days later, the Grays recaptured first place. On that same day, Adrian Constantine Anson boarded a train for Marshalltown, Iowa. The Chicago captain was returning to his father's house to die.

Spalding named Flint the interim captain, and the

Whites rallied around their new leader to keep apace of the Grays. On the first day of September, they were only a half game behind Providence and on their way to Rhode Island for a showdown series with George Wright's nine. It wasn't much of a three-game set as Providence scored in double figures each day while Chicago's best run total was three in the last game. When the Whites left town, the pennant race was over for them.

Syracuse folded during the second week of September, which affected the standings dramatically when only their first six games against each team were counted. This brought Buffalo back into the fray but only for a few days. Providence soon wrapped up the pennant. The White Stockings finished fourth.

At the same time that the Stars were calling it quits, Spalding released George Shaffer, calling him an unsettling influence on the club. The truth was much darker than that. Shaffer was being paid top dollar to play in Chicago, but the Whites were now out of the pennant race. Lew Brown was available, having been released by Providence the month before, and Brown would play out the last month of the season for much less than Shaffer. Spalding showed just how niggardly he could be and would be when he felt the situation was right.

Shortly thereafter, Anson wired that he had finally broken into a real hard sweat and was feeling better, confident that he was on the road to recovery. Wags in Chicago said that "chinner" Shaffer had caused Anson's illness with his incessant chatter, and now that "The Orator" was gone, Cap was sure to regain his health.

Anson did recover and rejoined the team as it journeyed west to California to play a series of exhibitions against local nines and a Cincinnati team that accompanied the White Stockings on the barnstorming tour. By the time they all returned that fall, Anson was in the pink of health and ready for the 1880 season.

11

Long Live the King!

Abe Lincoln and Congress put an end to slavery in the 1860s, then William Ambrose Hulbert and the other owners in the National League revived the "peculiar institution" at the end of the 1870s — but in a different form.

Dating back to the days before the National Association of Professional Base Ball Players was formed in '71, every player was free to choose the team for which he wished to play, providing the club he chose also wanted him and offered him a contract. For instance, John Doe wanted to play for Philadelphia and Philadelphia wanted him. Simple enough. Philadelphia would offer Doe a contract, and he would sign it and play for Philadelphia. The trouble was a good player's services would be desired by more than one club. Maybe New York also wanted Doe, so New York would offer him a bigger contract, even though he had already signed with Philadelphia and had accepted an advance on his salary. There was nothing to prevent Doe from signing with New York except his honor, which wasn't much of a barrier because many ballplayers of that era had no personal integrity whatsoever. The best Philadelphia could do was to demand the advance money returned and then hope to get it either from Doe or the New York club.

When a player did this, it was called "revolving" from one team to another. It was anything but kosher, but there was little legal recourse for the clubs until they made it a rule that no player could sign with one team then change his mind and contract with another for the same season. This didn't totally stop players from revolving, but it did stop the clubs from encouraging them to do it.

Gradually, as professional baseball became stablized by ethical men who wrote stricter rules and lived by them, revolving came to an end. The players weren't exactly happy about it, so they put themselves on the auction block, offering themselves to the highest bidder. The owners played the players' game until it proved financially ruinous as in '78 when the magnates put salary caps on themselves and standardized contracts throughout the National League. It was a fairly good idea, but it did have its drawbacks in that each club had to police itself, making certain that they didn't spend thousands of dollars on a handful of players and leave only token sums available for the rest of the squad.

When the Syracuse Stars disbanded in early September '79, Hulbert decided the time had come to restore slavery or at least a form of it. He called his fellow magnates together on September 30, and they voted his plan into National League law.

Quite simply, the owners approved the very first reserve clause for the players in which each team could reserve the services of five players currently under contract for the next season. No other team could sign or even contact players on the reserve list of another club, but all other players became free agents when their current contracts expired in the fall. This was fine for the lesser players of the day, but it meant bondage to the stars, the men baseball fanatics had come to admire and, in the case of a large number of ladies, desire. For the owners, it was an improvement on their operations, especially on their payrolls.

Using the new five-man reserve system, Spalding kept Joe Quest, Ned Williamson, George Gore, Abner Dalrymple, and Silver Flint for the '80 season. Captain Adrian Anson didn't need to be put on Chicago's reserve list because he was a stockholder in the Chicago Ball Club and thus an owner which meant he couldn't play for another team — even if he wanted to — as long as he held stock in the White Stockings. Newcomers to the squad were Mike "King" Kelly, Tommy Burns, Larry Corcoran, and Fred Goldsmith.

The acquisition of Kelly and Goldsmith wasn't exactly kosher. Kelly had played for Cincinnati in '79. Goldsmith had pitched for Troy during part of the season, then was released at the end of the campaign. The Cincinnati club's management resigned at the end of the playing season, and the stockholders asked Hulbert to run the club until they could choose a new management team. Hulbert agreed, and while he was running the club, he signed Goldsmith to a Cincinnati contract and put him on the reserve list with Kelly. Then *the stockholders* folded the club in early November, making Kelly and Goldsmith free agents.

Before telling the rest of the League magnates that Cincinnati's reserved men were now available, Hulbert wasted no time in signing Kelly and Goldsmith to sizeable contracts with the White Stockings.

Of course, O.P. Caylor of the Cincinnati *Enquirer* screamed highway robbery, saying in no uncertain terms that Hulbert and his Chicago gang had murdered the Cincinnati club, then looted the corpse. Caylor was overreacting as he was wont to do. He was somewhat mollified when the Star Club of Syracuse reorganized and moved to the Ohio River city for the 1880 campaign.

While Hulbert and Spalding were maneuvering in the front office, Cap Anson had joined the '79 squad on a barnstorming tour of Iowa, Nebraska, Salt Lake City, and California. This was the first of several postseason playing trips for Chicago teams.

At the winter meetings in Niagara Falls, New York, the rules committee made three significant changes in the game. The first was reducing the number of balls necessary for a free pass to first base from nine down to eight. The second required the catcher to catch the third strike on a batter before it hit the ground or risk allowing the hitter the opportunity to reach first ahead of his throw. The last of the changes was in the game itself.

For as long as anyone could remember, a coin toss or some other means of chance decided which team would bat first and who would take the field first. Then both teams would go to the bat nine times each, regardless of the score when the team that was batting last came to bat in the bottom of the ninth. For the 1880 season, if the team to bat last was ahead going into the bottom of the ninth, then that team no longer had to bat; the game was over.

With the Cincinnati club folded and the reorganized Star Club moving from Syracuse to Cincinnati, the National League was left with only seven teams at the time of the Niagara Falls confab. The only serious applicant for the vacancy was the Worcester, Massachusetts club. The established magnates voted them into the League unanimously although reluctantly. The 1880 season would see the National League made up of teams from Boston, Buffalo, Chicago, Cincinnati, Cleveland, Providence, Troy, and Worcester.

The early line on the season had the sportswriters pegging Providence to repeat as NL champs, in spite of the fact that George Wright was balking about playing in the Rhode Island capital again. Boston was picked for second, and the White Stockings were begrudgingly tagged for third.

Larry Corcoran stepped into the pitcher's box for the opening game in Cincinnati against the Stars on May 1, 1880, and when the sun set that day, the 20–year–old right–handed fireballer from Brooklyn had his first Major League victory, 4–3. The White Stockings won their second game, lost the third two days later, then began rolling like a juggernaut that only a few teams could slow down but never completely halt.

A typical game during this stretch was played on May 7 when the Whites mauled Providence, 20–7, behind Corcoran. George Gore had six singles in as many tries that day.

Over the next four weeks, Chicago won 12 straight to jump off to a 14–1 start before Harry Wright's Boston nine dumped the Whites in a game that Anson protested from the start because Boston used George Wright, who was on Providence's reserve list, at shortstop. This was the first test of the reserve agreement, and it was the first time Anson played a game under protest.

Anson later withdrew the complaint, but Hulbert wasn't so forgiving with Wright. George was told that if he wanted to play baseball in the National League he would have to do so with the Providence club until such time that he was released by that organization.

Many years later Anson wrote that Larry Corcoran "had the endurance of an Indian pony." He must not have thought so in 1880 because when the Whites were scheduled to play two days in a row Corcoran would pitch the first day and Fred Goldsmith would throw the next. Harry Wright created the first pitching rotation with his '76 Red Stockings when he alternated starts by his pitchers, but this was the first time Chicago had anything resembling a pitching rotation.

Fred Goldsmith was the same man who in 1870 was credited with proving that a baseball could be made to follow an elliptical path during a demonstration that was allegedly witnessed by the inimitable Henry Chadwick. Hailing from New Haven, Connecticut, Goldsmith played on three different New England clubs and one in Canada before signing with Troy late in the '79 season, posting an unremarkable record of 2–4 in seven starts.

During this day of iron–fisted men who played the game with their bare hands, the position of catcher was the most dangerous because chest protectors, masks, and shin guards were either unheard of or seldom used. Because of this, the man who played behind the place usually had a short career unless he played on a team that had a good change catcher.* Silver Flint's playing days would have been considerably shorter if not for Michael

---

* A change catcher was a player who was already in the game who would change positions with the regular catcher at some point in the game, usually when the regular catcher's hands became too painful to play the position any longer. A substitute catcher was another catcher on the bench who substituted for the regular catcher from game to game, thus giving the regular catcher a day off now and then.

Joseph Kelly, also known as King Kelly.

Mike Kelly was the consummate ballplayer of the 19th century. He could play several positions with equally great skill; he was handsome; and he was personable. The native of Troy, N.Y., had but one serious fault: he loved to pull the cork. He was just beginning to blossom on the diamond when Hulbert signed him at Anson's insistance. His first two seasons in the National League had been spent with the Cincinnati club where he hit .283 in '78 and .348 in '79. Besides being an excellent hitter, he could run with the best of them, and when he was sober, he was an outstanding fielder. Kelly was usually behind the plate when Goldsmith was in the pitcher's box.

While Corcoran and Goldsmith were mowing down opposing hitters from the middle of the diamond, Chicago's offense was driving the opposition to total distraction. Gore and Dalrymple had been excellent base-runners before the arrival of Kelly, but when the daring Irishman joined the squad, he and the White Stockings brought a whole new approach to the game. Speed could win games, and Anson's gang of base thieves set out to prove it.

Although stolen base records weren't being kept yet, nearly every newspaper article about Chicago's games mentioned how someone or everyone on the White Stockings managed to swipe a base here or there that aided in that day's victory. The Whites were also adept at stretching singles into doubles, doubles into triples, and triples into homers.

By the first week in June, the White Stockings had built a four-game lead over Cleveland and were in Providence for a series with the Rhode Islanders. The contest of June 4 turned out to be a real humdinger.

With the score tied in the bottom of the 17th inning, Ned Williamson slammed a pitch between the outfielders and raced around to third base. Due up were Anson, Kelly, and Corcoran who was almost as mean with a stick as he was with the ball. Seeing that the game was probably lost, Providence's captain, John Montgomery Ward, approached the umpire and requested that the game be called on account of darkness. Anson argued that there was at least a half hour of daylight left. The ump jawed at both men, and by the time they all quit jabbering at each other, darkness was imminent. The game was called and had to be replayed in its entirety. Ward could have saved his breath because the Whites won the makeup game anyway.

Chicago started a winning streak during that first week in June that lasted into the second week of July. After those two straight losses to Boston on May 29 and 31, the White Stockings reeled off 21 consecutive victories, racing to a 35–3 mark and a 13½–game lead over second place Providence. Cleveland's Jim McCormick, the hefty Scot from Glasgow, finally brought the win skein to an end on July 10 by shutting out the Whites, 2–0, in Cleveland. At this time, three Chicagoans were high up on the hitting ladder, and one was leading the league.

Rookie Tommy Burns started out life in Honesdale, Pennsylvania on March 30, 1857. His pro baseball career began with Hornell in the National Association in 1878. Spalding saw him playing at Albany, and although he wasn't yet much of a hitter, he was a slick fielder, and every team could use a good shortstop. In the middle of the 1880 campaign, he was rocking the NL with a .386 batting average and was getting good support from George Gore at .351 and Abner Dalrymple at .324.

By the fourth week of July, it appeared that nothing

could stop the White Stockings from winning the flag that had eluded them in '79. Then Goldsmith came down with chills and a fever on the night of July 22. Taking no chances, Hulbert immediately sent him home and told him to stay there until he was well. To replace him, Spalding signed Tom Poorman who was pitching for a team in Pennsylvania. Anson, afraid to put a rookie in the pitcher's box during the middle of the campaign, decided Corcoran would have to carry the team until either his arm fell off or Goldsmith returned, which ever should occur first.

Finally coming to his senses, Anson gave Poorman a chance, and the rookie pitcher responded by winning two games without a defeat. It was 21 games later that Goldsmith was well enough to return to the team.

After their 21–game winning streak came to a halt in Cleveland, the Whites lost three of their next eight games.

Feeling responsible and wishing to get his boys going again, Anson pulled an unprecedented move when he fined himself for lackadaisical play on July 24. It didn't help much as the Whites lost four of their next nine contests. Fortunately, none of the trailing nines could make up any ground on them. On August 14, Chicago still held a 12½–game lead over Providence and a 13–game gap over Cleveland.

With only six weeks left in the season and a pennant for Chicago reasonably assured, Hulbert turned his attention to League matters. Word had it that the Cincinnati Stars were permitting other teams to use their grounds for Sunday games and that beer was being sold at these local affairs. This was strictly against NL policy — really Hulbert's policy — but not its rules. O.P. Caylor cast down the gauntlet when he warned Hulbert in the

Cincinnati *Enquirer* that if the League didn't keep its hands off Sunday games and beer in Cincinnati he would personally lead a crusade against Hulbert, the National League, and the reserve agreement, even forming a new league if that was what it took to prove his point that beer at the ball park and games on Sunday wouldn't ruin the game. Hulbert let Caylor have his say, deciding to wait until the season was over before acting.

A week after Caylor's tirade against the big league appeared in print, his precious Cincinnati team was eliminated from the race along with the Buffalo Bison. Three days later, Boston and Worcester were out of the race as well. Then Flint took a foul off his throwing hand and had to sit out a while. Fortunately, Anson had Kelly to replace him.

On September 2, the White Stockings played their first ever doubleheader, necessitated by a rainout the day before and the fact that Troy couldn't stay in Chicago an extra day to make up the game. To make certain that the club got as much as it could from the rearranged schedule, Hulbert had the first game played in the morning and the second in the late afternoon, closing down the park between games for lunch. The Whites won the first game, 1–0, but lost the night cap, 5–1. Troy was eliminated two days later, and that left only Providence and Cleveland in the race with Chicago.

Goldsmith recovered from his illness and returned to the team on September 6, just in time for Cleveland to bow out of the pennant struggle. Poorman was released but went to Buffalo where he completed the season. Nine days later, Chicago dumped Cincinnati, 5–2, in Ohio, while Boston was beating Providence.

And for the second time in five years, the Chicago White Stockings were champs of the National League.

1880 was a great year for the White Stockings individually and as a team. George Gore won the batting title with a .360 average. Anson hit .337; Dalrymple .330; and Tommy Burns .309. Larry Corcoran won 43 games while losing only 14; threw a no–hitter against Boston on August 19; had five shutouts; pitched 536 innings; and struck out an incredible 268 batters, which was a League record for the next four years. Fred Goldsmith had a 21–3 record with an ERA of 1.75. Chicago won 67 out of 84 games for a winning percentage of .798, a mark that may stay in the baseball record book for eternity. The White Stockings also led the League in hitting and fielding. They scored an unbelieveable 6.4 runs per game, which, if stretched out over a 162–game schedule, would be a total 1,036 for a late 20th century team.

All things considered the performance of the 1880 Chicago White Stockings may have been the best ever by any Major League team in the history of the game.

12

Encore '81

Purists cry every time baseball's rules are changed or someone comes up with an equipment innovation. Usually, the press leads the chorus, screaming in print, "Leave the game alone."

Fortunately, the press doesn't have as much power over the game as it likes to think.

One experiment after another was tried by the baseball experts throughout the 1870s. The rules were altered every year, and each time they were the game was improved. Different balls were tried; a lively ball, a dead ball, a mushy ball, etc. Gloves were just becoming a part of a player's equipment although only some catchers and a few firstbasemen were using them. Masks and chest protectors were just coming into vogue.

The style of play was changing, too. Basemen were finally playing off their respective bags. Pitchers were discovering that a ball could be made to curve, drop, and rise and that variations in speed of delivery could be as effective as the fastest of fast balls. Base–stealing was discovered to be a very effective offensive weapon.

Experimentation continued into the 1880s.

With the invention of the electric light and carbon arc lamps of considerable power, the promoters of these contrivances cast their eyes on baseball. The Boston press was invited to Nantasket Beach, Massachusetts on September 2, 1880 to see the first trial of night baseball. Three hundred spectators crowded onto the balconies of the Sea Foam House on Strawberry Hill. 36 carbon lamps, 12 to a group atop each of three 100–foot high towers, were placed 500 feet apart, overlooking a tri–angular area that contained the playing diamond. Be–tween 8:00 and 9:30 p.m. Nine innings of baseball were played between the employee teams of Jordan, Marsh & Co., and R.H. White & Co. The Boston journalists weren't impressed and wrote that the idea of playing baseball under lights was impractical.

The White Stockings got into the experimentation act immediately after the close of the 1880 regular playing season.

In the first of a pair of exhibitions with the Buffalo Bisons, the two teams tried using a "square" bat, i.e., a cricket bat that had two flat sides on its business end. Not one man liked the idea, complaining that each time the ball was hit on an edge that it stung like a swarm of bees. The bat didn't last the game, but the cricket ball they used did. Even so, the players preferred the Spalding ball.

The next day the two teams tried playing with a few rules that were designed to speed up play. The first was lowering the number of balls needed for a walk from eight to six. The second was the elimination of the "fair ball" warning to hitters with two strikes on them. The third change was meant to prevent dallying on the bases by runners when a foul ball was hit. A runner could be thrown out trying to get back to the base he had left if the fielder could retrieve a foul ball and return it to the pitcher who could then throw it to the baseman for the tag.

The Chicago press and all the players liked the proposed rule changes.

A special meeting of the League was ordered by Hulbert for October 4, 1880 in Rochester with all the clubs represented.

O.P. Caylor blasted Hulbert in the Cincinnati *Enquirer* for calling the conference because its express purpose was the censure of the Cincinnati Stars for selling beer on their playing grounds and for renting their park to other teams on Sundays. At the outset of the confab, H.F. Root of Providence presented an amendment to Section 7 of Article 5 of the League constitution that dealt with the clubs playing Sunday games. Root's proposal restricted a club from allowing "any game of ball to be played on its grounds on Sunday" and it would forbid the "sale of every description of malt, spiritous or vinous liquors on the club grounds" and called for the expulsion of the perpetrator. Seven club representatives immediately voted for and signed a document agreeing to Root's amendments.

Naturally, the Cincinnati man, W.C. Kennett, emphatically opposed the amendment, stating that Sunday rentals and beer sales brought in good revenue that was needed for the club's basic survival. Hulbert insisted that Kennett wire the directors of the Cincinnati club and inform them of the amendments, and Kennett did after telling Hulbert that it was useless because the directors would stand behind his decision. Kennett was right, and the other members of the NL declared Cincinnati's place to be open; in effect, expelling Cincinnati.

The only other piece of business for the conferees was the readoption of the reserve clause. Buffalo and Boston opposed the renewal of the pact until the Red Stockings were *bought off* by Hulbert when he permitted them to retain Charles "Pop" Snyder who wanted to leave for Washington. Buffalo then stood alone and was outvoted, 6–1.

Caylor was incensed at Hulbert and the other NL magnates for expelling Cincinnati and upholding the reserve clause. His ire reached such magnitude that he called for the formation of a new league to compete with the established circuit. He even went so far as to announce a meeting of prospective owners to be held in New York on November 4. The conference never came off, and Caylor's plans were put into mothballs for the time being.

At the annual winter meeting of the National League at the St. James Hotel in New York in December, 1880, Detroit was admitted to the League to replace Cincinnati and a few rule changes were made. The pitcher's box was moved back five feet. The number of balls needed for a walk was reduced to seven, and the "Fair ball" warning was done away with. Although he declined to be a candidate for the presidency again, Hulbert was re-elected to the post and Nick Young was also retained as secretary-treasurer.

For the first time in their history, the White Stockings were able to retain the entire starting nine from one season to the next. Flint, Anson, Quest, Burns, Williamson, Dalrymple, Gore, Kelly, and both starting pitchers, Corcoran and Goldsmith, signed on for '81. The players who lived in Chicago during the winter held regular workouts at the Athenaeum Gymnasium under the watchful eye of Cap Anson. By the time they were ready to move outdoors in April, Anson had them in top condition and ready to start the season.

Cleveland was the opening day opponent for the Whites on April 30, 1881, in Chicago, and the home team came away winners, 8–5, in spite of a serious "jangle" between Cleveland's captain Mike McGeary and the umpire. The White Stockings split their next four contests and found themselves trailing Worcester by two games at the end of the first week of action.

The highlight of the second week's action was the first defeat of the year for Worcester, administered to them by the Whites and Hulbert's dog. In the seventh inning, little Tommy Burns, far from being a slugger, sent the ball to the clubhouse in the left field corner of White Stocking Park. Hulbert's big black dog was sleeping on the platform outside the president's office. As the ball rolled up to the beast, Worcester leftfielder Louis Pessano "Buttercup" Dickerson stopped short and refused to go near the animal. The dog simply continued to lie there, minding his own business, while Burns circled the bases for a homer. Worcester made a "silly protest" of interference by the dog, but the umpire overruled them and the homer was allowed to stand.

At the end of three weeks of play, Worcester continued to lead the League standings with a 10–3 mark to Chicago's 9–5. Boston, Buffalo, and Providence were all over .500 and in the next three positions in the standings, in that order.

When the Red Stockings came to town the third week, secondbaseman Jack Burdock protested the presence of Hulbert's dog in the playing area and demanded the removal of the animal. He also complained about the clubhouse doors being open and should be closed lest some Chicago player's hit roll through the opening, allowing him to a home run. Hulbert replied, "There's no rule covering dogs and doors, but if it will make you happier, the dog shall be bounced and the door closed." The gain made by Burdock didn't help his teammates against the White Stockings. "The dangerous Bostons and their phenomenal pitcher were taken into camp, 5 to 4," reported the *Tribune*. "Dare devil baserunning of Kelly did the trick." It was strongly suspected that Kelly, in his eagerness to reach home plate from second base, somehow forgot about third, slighting that bag entirely by 15 feet, thereby saving as much time and distance. Umpire Alfred Barker, of necessity, was fixing his attention on first base where Boston was disposing of Anson who had hit a grounder to second. Barker couldn't possibly have known whether Kelly touched third or not, so he allowed the run to stand in spite of Boston's protest. Williamson added icing to the cake by breaking up a Boston rally in the ninth with the hidden ball trick on Burdock to the Bostonian's immense discomfort and the delight of the Chicago fans.

After sweeping three straight from Boston, the Whites took over first place on May 25 with an 11–6 victory over Providence. Two days later their six–game win skein was halted by the same Grays, but Chicago remained in first place. Two weeks later Buffalo moved into a tie with the White Stockings as each team sported 15–9 records, but it was only temporary. Chicago resumed leadership of the National League a few days later.

June 25, 1881 was a remarkable day for George Gore. He had three hits, scored five runs, and stole seven bases as he led the Whites to a 12–8 win over Providence at Lakefront Park.

The Whites won their 10th in a row to improve their record to 26–10 on July 2 building a five–game lead over Buffalo in the process. Even so, they weren't the news of the day because a crazed assassin shot President James Garfield on that same day.

There was talk of cancelling games until the president's doctors pronounced his condition as being serious but stable. Assured that Garfield was okay for the time being, Hulbert gave approval for the schedule to continue.

An estimated crowd of over 10,000 turned out for the White Stockings' 4th of July celebration against the Boston Red Stockings. As usual on Independence Day, the weather was very hot in Chicago. So were the Bean Eaters as they snapped the Whites' winning streak, 11–10. "The pampered children should finish the game in less than two hours," wrote one Chicago scribe, "and complain less about the heat; thousands of farm laborers, bricklayers and laborers work in the sun all day with constant danger of sun stroke. Spectators were hot and impatient of delays."

Two weeks later Anson's gang lost five in a row, three of the defeats coming in Buffalo to the second place Bisons. They finally won a game, then promptly lost two more as their lead dwindled to two and a half games over the oncoming Bisons.

The memory of the '79 season was still fresh in everybody's mind, and the newspapers began crying that the sky was falling again.

The truth of the matter was Larry Corcoran wasn't having the same sort of season he'd had in 1880; he had a sore arm. Goldsmith was also less effective than he was in 1880. The hitting was there with Anson pounding out an average of .450 through the middle of July. He wasn't alone as Flint sported an average of .372; Kelly's was .359; Gore's .312; Dalrymple's .311; and Burns' .300.

Then Corcoran's arm quit hurting, and the Whites

reeled off four straight wins at home; three of them over Buffalo. When the White Stockings played their final home game of the season on August 25, they had an eight-game lead over Buffalo. The players celebrated the season by giving Hulbert a gold watch and chain with a locket attached containing a picture of the 12 donors, which was worth $200.

President Garfield had rallied and relapsed on several occasions since being shot July 2, but he finally succumbed to the assassin's bullets on September 18. It was learned during the autopsy that he died of internal bleeding caused by an abscess that was caused by a bullet which the doctors had failed to detect and remove.

The next day, September 19, 1881, the Whites clinched their second straight pennant when Troy beat Buffalo, 7–5. Hulbert ordered a day of mourning for Garfield to coincide with the president's funeral. Confusion about which day that would be arose, and some of the teams didn't know what to do, especially the Troy club. When the day of Garfield's interment came, the White Stockings were in New York to play the Trojans. Anson wasn't sure of what to do except play when the Troy management insisted on it. Hulbert was embarrassed but did nothing except chastise the men of Troy. He would have been equally justified for calling the Troy management on the carpet for playing their last game of the season on September 27, also against Chicago, in a driving rainstorm, especially when the attendance was a record low of 12.

Individually, the '81 season was excellent for several Chicago players. Besides being the captain (manager) of the best team in the League, Anson won the batting title with a .399 average, led the NL in RBIs with 82 and hits with 137, and he led all firstbasemen in fielding average, putouts, and assists. Kelly and Dalrymple each hit .323, and Flint wound up at .310. Larry Corcoran, in spite of his mid–season slump, managed to win 31 games to lead the League.

It was such a great year that every single man on the roster signed a new contract for '82 on or before October 9. The rest of the National League was put on notice right then: the White Stockings aimed to make it three pennants in a row in '82.

13

Three–Time Winners

"There are no great men, only great challenges that ordinary men are forced by circumstances to meet." Admiral William F. "Bull" Halsey was the author of that quote. He could have been talking about William Ambrose Hulbert who met the challenge of bringing professional baseball back to respectability at a time when it was close to descending to the depths of the underworld.

Hulbert called another special meeting of National League magnates at the Adelphi Hotel in Saratoga, New York for September 29, 1881. The purpose of the conference was to establish a blacklist of players, managers, and umpires who were guilty of "dissipation and general insubordination." This new group of banned men would join the gamblers of the 1870s who were similarly expelled from the League. They would also be denied employment by NL teams but not permanently. Upon application by the banned player and unanimous consent of the League at the annual meeting, a man could be reinstated.

While the National League was acting, other forces were afoot, led by O.P. Caylor of Cincinnati. Caylor had a non–League team that he called the Cincinnati Reds, and he took them to several different cities to play in the summer of 1881. Among their opponents were the St. Louis Browns, Philadelphia Athletics, Pittsburgh, Louisville, and Baltimore. All of these teams played on Sundays and sold beer at their ball parks. A meeting of their leaders was called for early November in Cincinnati.

When word reached Hulbert that the "Sunday–Beer" forces had finally rallied together, the National League president became so enraged that he was absolutely apoplectic and was confined to his bed on October 29. It was later determined that he had suffered a mild heart attack.

As Hulbert recuperated at his home, Caylor's group met in Cincinnati and formed the American Association. The new loop's organizers were Caylor, Aaron Stern, Louis Kramer, and Louis Herancourt of Cincinnati; Denny McKnight and Horace B. Phillips of Pittsburgh; Billy Barnie of Baltimore; Charles Mason, Lew Simmons, and Billy Sharsig of Philadelphia; Chris Von Der Ahe, W.W. Judy, and A.H. Spink of St. Louis; and J.W. Reccius and John Botto of Louisville.

Of course, the National League ignored this new threat at their winter meetings at Chicago's Tremont House in December 1881. Instead, the NL magnates confined themselves to routine business, such as changing some playing rules and upholding their blacklist decree of September. One strange item that was totally asinine but driven through by Hulbert in order to help his friend Spalding was the adoption by the League of the "Spalding uniform". As he had done with the White Stockings, Spalding proposed that every team wear uniforms that were color–co–ordinated by position. The only distinguishing mark from team to team would be the color of their stockings. Chicago would wear white, of course; Cleveland, dark blue; Providence, light blue; Worcester, brown; Buffalo, gray; Troy, green; Boston, red; and Detroit, yellow. All pants and ties would be white, but shirts, belts, and caps would be prescribed as follows, each club using the same colors:

Catcher	scarlet
Pitcher	light blue
Firstbaseman	scarlet and white
Secondbaseman	orange and blue
Thirdbaseman	blue and white
Shortstop	maroon
Leftfielder	white
Centerfielder	red and black
Rightfielder	gray
Substitute	green and brown

Spalding was turning baseball into a circus, and everyone was going along with him as witnessed by the uniforms of nearly every team in the nation in future years.

Hulbert remained confined to his sick bed throughout the winter. At times, he felt well enough to rise and did on occasion but never left his home. When Anson and the boys began their spring exercising, the Chicago club's president wanted to go watch them work out, but his doctor warned against any unnecessary exertion. Bill Hulbert wasn't one to listen to advice too often, even from a physician. Late in the afternoon of April 10, 1882, Hulbert tried to right himself in bed, clasped his chest, announced to his servant and nurse that he was having extreme pain in his chest, then collapsed on his pillow. William Ambrose Hulbert, founder and president of the National League of Base Ball Clubs and president of the Chicago Ball Club, was dead at the age of 49.

Two days later the club's stockholders held a memorial meeting to honor their late leader, and on April 14, Hulbert was buried in Graceland Cemetery, only two blocks from where Wrigley Field would be built three decades later. His headstone was most unique in that it was the shape of a baseball mounted on crossed bats.

Spalding and John L. Walsh bought up Hulbert's shares in the club from his widow, and on April 26, 1882, the stockholders elected Spalding to the presidency and a new board of directors that included Chicago Board of Trade members Walsh, John Lyon, and Charles T. Trego. Spalding and Walsh were now the principal owners of the team.

With Hulbert gone, something went out of the White Stockings. It was mostly Anson's spirit. Like Spalding, Anson had gotten very close to Hulbert, so close that Anson relied on Hulbert for advice and direction on how to handle the team. When this was denied him, Anson felt somewhat insecure as the team's leader, and it showed during the early weeks of the '82 campaign.

The White Stockings began the season on the road, playing all of the other western teams a series each. Every club was out to get the champions from Chicago, and they would stop at nothing to beat the Whites. Buffalo went so far as to slope their basepaths so the Chicagoans would have to run slightly uphill from base to base. The effect was more psychological than physical. In Cleveland, a fan hit Anson in the back of the head with a seat cushion. Anson grabbed a bat and sought the culprit, being guided by another Cleveland spectator in the direction the villain had taken. Anse pushed his way through the departing crowd, grabbed a man by the shoulder, spun him around, took hold of his coat lapel, and prepared to put out the gent's lights with a Baltimore chop. Fortunately, the White Stockings' captain realized in time that he had the wrong man, released him, and offered a quick apology. The incident only served to further unnerve Cap. After three weeks of play, the White Stockings were in fifth place with a 6–5 record.

After the Whites played in Detroit, the newspapers from both cities ran stories that questioned Anson's ability to manage without Hulbert present to back him up. The Detroit paper said it appeared to them that Anse "was losing control of the team." The *Tribune* reiterated this statement on May 28, stating as fact that Anson had less control of the team because Hulbert was no longer around to make certain decisions and suggestions concerning the team.

There must have been some truth to this report because on June 17 the Whites were still wallowing in fifth with a 13–14 mark, five games behind frontrunner Providence. A *Tribune* writer sounded the death knell, pronouncing the Whites as good as dead in the '82 pennant race.

Someone forgot to relay that message to the team. The week after the "death notice" the Whites had a five-game winning streak and slipped past Troy into fourth with a 17–15 record. After a loss to Providence, they went on another five-game winning binge, beating Providence twice and Boston thrice to move themselves into third place at 22–15 a game behind Providence and Detroit who were tied for first.

Detroit took control of first place on July 3 with a win over Troy, while Buffalo was dumping Providence. Chicago won for the sixth straight time on the same day, then made it eight in a row on Independence Day with a morning-afternoon twinbill sweep of Troy at home. Detroit split a doubleheader with Boston, and the two western teams found themselves deadlocked for the lead with 25–15 records. When the Michigan nine lost to Boston on the sixth, the White Stockings were left alone on top of the National League. It wasn't a permanent perch.

The holiday doubleheader with Troy drew 19,000 "cranks" — as fans were being called in the '80s — for the split fare. This total represented almost two–thirds of Boston's total attendance for the previous year. Troy's cut of the gate amounted to approximately $2,800; enough to pay three players for the season.

Chicago's winning streak ended at 10, and the Whites lost two in a row the following week but held on to first. The spirit was back in the team as evidenced by the accusation that George Gore maliciously spiked a Troy player. Gore denied the charge, of course; and Anson defended his player to the hilt. The umpire sided with the Chicagoans.

Anson was the definite cause of this resurrection. The *Tribune* writer noted how the Whites' captain swore "certain obscenities" at his players from the bench when they made mistakes on the basepaths, and he jawed at them nose–to–nose when they miscued in the field. Cap didn't just lead with his lip though; he matched his irascible verbosity with his play in the game. He led the League in hitting in early July with a .397 average and was still holding up with a .389 mark a month later.

The summer heat did odd things to the White Stockings. They couldn't win more than two or three games at a time, and just as often as they would win thrice, they would turn around and drop a pair. When the Whites did come away victorious, it was usually by a very lopsided score. On July 14, Gore, Kelly, and Williamson each had three RBIs and three runs scored as Chicago dumped

Detroit, 23–4, at home. 10 days later they went on a bigger rampage against Cleveland as Dalrymple, Gore, Kelly, Williamson, Nicol, Flint, and Burns collected four hits apiece enroute to a 35–4 massacre.

When Providence regained first place from the Whites in early August, rebellion broke out on the Chicago nine. Ned Williamson voiced his anger with Anson over being fined, stating unequivocally in the newspapers that he wanted to play in Detroit in '83.

Williamson wasn't alone in his dissatisfaction with Anson. Mike Kelly, Joe Quest, and Tommy Burns had their positions switched on them. In an attempt to gain more consistency from his team, Anson experimented with his lineup by moving Kelly to short, Quest to right, and Burns to second. The result was poor play and more losses. Providence improved its lead over Chicago, stretching the gap to three games on September 2. To make matters worse, Boston, Detroit, Cleveland, and Buffalo were all slowly moving up on the White Stockings. With a month to go, six teams still had excellent chances of winning the pennant.

Anson came to his senses at the right time. On September 5, he moved Kelly, Quest, and Burns back to their normal places on the field. To bring them luck, the team discarded the red caps with the accompanying stripes of color to denote positions that Spalding had them wearing that year and returned to the tri–colored caps of the previous two seasons. The change must have worked because the Whites mauled Troy, 10–0, that day to start one of the most fantastic finishes in the game's history.

On September 9, the White Stockings shellacked Troy, 24–1, for their third straight win. Gore, Anson, Kelly, Burns, and Flint each had four hits, and Corcoran threw a three–hitter in the eight–inning game that was shortened by darkness.

Three days later Harry Wright's Providence nine came to town, still sporting a three–game lead. The Whites won the first game, 6–4, to narrow the gap to two, eliminating Cleveland from the pennant race at the same time. The next day Anson went 3–for–4 as the White Stockings eked out another victory, 6–5, in spite of Wright's protest that Kelly had cheated by interfering with brother George's throwing at shortstop on a crucial play.

In the third game of the set, Fred Goldsmith stepped into the pitcher's box and held the Grays to a pair of tallies. At the same time, he pounded out two doubles and knocked in four runs to lead the Whites to a 6–2 win and into first place by percentage points.

On September 16, the White Stockings won their seventh straight by downing Worcester, 5–1. Anson left the team immediately after the game, taking an express train for Philadelphia. Virginia Anson had gone back to her parents' home to give birth to the Ansons' first child, a son, that Anson would be seeing for the first time. The visit was short but sweet.

Cap returned to Chicago in time to play the next game on Tuesday the 19th, and the Whites whipped Worcester again, 13–5, eliminating Detroit from the pennant race. The next day, in what was supposed to have been the White Stockings' final *scheduled* home game, Corcoran pitched a 5–0 no–hitter against the last place club, knocking Boston and Buffalo out of the race.

Providence was still very much alive though, only a game back having lost two more games than Chicago.

The White Stockings headed east for the final week of the season to play a three–game set with Cleveland and a quartet of contests with Buffalo. Providence had five games left, including three at home against hapless Worcester and a pair with Troy.

The Whites hadn't been very successful in either Lake Erie city, while Providence had had nothing but good luck against the League's bottom two teams. The gamblers were giving narrow odds that the Grays would overcome the Whites during the campaign's final days.

As the Whites prepared to play Cleveland, a special meeting of the National League's magnates was being held in Philadelphia.

A.H. Soden, the Boston club's president who had become acting-president of the circuit upon Hulbert's death, called the meeting at Spalding's request. Two important items were set before the club representatives.

One concerned realignment of the League, and the other was Spalding's request that the final three games scheduled between his White Stockings and the Bison in Buffalo be switched to Chicago. Troy and Worcester, the two worst teams and also the two smallest cities, were asked to resign from the National League so teams from New York and Philadelphia could be admitted. The other six teams were being nice about it by asking the pair to withdraw because they could easily vote to revoke their memberships. Troy and Worcester didn't like it, but they agreed.

The rescheduling matter was against League rules, but Spalding argued that it was necessary because attendance would be much better in Chicago which would give Buffalo a bigger take than if they played at home. And Buffalo needed the money. When Soden called for the question, the vote was 7–1 in favor of shifting the series to Chicago. The only dissenting ballot was cast by

Providence, of course.

While the confab was happening in Philadelphia, Cleveland was pounding all over Goldsmith and the White Stockings, 15–6, on the shores of Lake Erie. Idle Providence moved to a half game behind and only one loss down. Corcoran pitched the next day, and his hot streak continued as he shut out Cleveland, 8–0, on a three–hitter. Providence also won, so nothing changed except the number of games left for each team to play.

On Monday the 25th, Corcoran took the mound again. George Gore tripled in the sixth inning of the scoreless game. Ned Williamson grounded out, but Gore's speed enabled him to score. Cleveland tied it up an inning later. Gore then walked in the eighth, stole second, then went to third on Williamson's single to center. Anson then grounded out, but it was enough to score Gore from third to make the final, 2–1.

Providence was splitting a doubleheader with Worcester at the same time, reducing the White Stockings' magic number to three.

The Whites shuffled off to Buffalo for a single contest on the 26th with their fate in their own hands. All they had to do was win three from the Bison and the '82 National League flag was theirs.

Trailing, 7–2, going into the bottom of the seventh, Chicago scored four big runs to narrow Buffalo's lead to 7–6. Joe Quest led off the bottom of the eighth with a walk, then moved to second on Silver Flint's single. Abner Dalrymple sacrificed both runners up a base, then Gore grounded out scoring Quest with the tying run. Williamson followed with an RBI single, and the White Stockings held on to win, 8–7, and cut the magic number down to two.

Both teams traveled to Chicago for the final three

games.

Providence needed a minor miracle to win the pennant. The White Stockings needed only a win or a Grays' loss to cinch a tie for the title. Two wins for Chicago or two losses by Providence or one Chicago victory and one Providence defeat would give the Whites their third straight National League championship.

Anson sent Larry Corcoran to the pitcher's box for the first game in the series, and the Chicago ace responded by holding Buffalo to a single tally in an 8–1 victory. Now assured of no less than a tie for the top spot, Anson called on Fred Goldsmith to put the final touch to a fantastic finish, and the veteran curveball specialist came through with an 11–5 win to clinch the pennant. Dalrymple and Kelly each had three hits, and Flint hit a two–run homer.

Chicago's baseball devotees were delirious that Thursday night as they celebrated their team's third straight title. It was rumored that Kelly began drinking within minutes of the last out and didn't stop until passing out the next night. True or false, it made no matter because Spalding used the occasion of the last win of the year on Saturday to announce that every man on the team except the little Scot, Hughie Nicol, had signed contracts for '83. With the pennant all wrapped up, Anson played with the lineup for the final game. He put 16–year–old Milton Scott at first, and the youngest player ever to suit up and play for the Cubs went 2–for–5. Ned Williamson had a perfect 5–for–5 day and scored the winning run in the 10th inning on Kelly's single. Corcoran won his 10th straight game as well.

The '82 campaign was filled with laurels for the White Stockings, just as the two previous seasons had been. Anson hit .362 to finish second to Dan Brouthers of Buffalo at .368. Cap was also second to Brouthers in hits with 126 to the big slugger's 129. Other .300–hitters on the Chicago nine were Gore at .319, and Kelly at .305.

Corcoran's 27–13 record gave him the best won–lost percentage in the NL at .675. He also had the lowest ERA at 1.95 and lowest hits per nine innings average at 7.11.

1882 was by far the best season the National League had ever had to that time. For the first time ever, six teams were still in the pennant race with less than a month to go in the season. With less than two weeks to go, five teams were still in contention.

1882 was also the best year yet for the Chicago Ball Club. Attendance in Chicago reached an all–time high of an estimated 130,000, and everyone agreed that if not for the enormous support received by the White Stockings some of the other clubs might not have survived the year. It was little wonder that Spalding was able to get his way concerning the late season schedule change.

14

The First Baseball Wars

Competition is good for business. Too much competition isn't.

When the magnates of the American Association (AA) set up shop in 1882, they did it with the idea of destroying the National League or forcing the NL to accept them. They didn't try to raid the NL for players, but actually did the opposite by working within the parameters of the established league's rules and practices.* The AA leaders merely offered baseball fans an alternative, and it turned out to be good for everyone.

The National League leaders wisely ignored the AA in the beginning, then stupidly went to war with the new circuit. Part of the reason for the NL taking such a position was Hulbert's death. The League was a little short on guidance in '82 under A.H. Soden of Boston because Soden was far from being the dynamic individual that Hulbert had been. Soden spent his time in office more as a caretaker than a leader, but that was good because few men could follow in Hulbert's footsteps. If Soden had tried to change the League to fit his tastes, he would have met with solid resistance from his

* The only real exceptions were the playing of games on Sundays and selling beer at the ball parks.

fellow owners, and this might have led to disunity and possibly even dissolution of the NL. Instead, the League's leaders rallied behind Soden and helped him through the difficult transition period between Hulbert's mortal departure and the next annual meeting in December 1882.

One of the problems the National League experienced during Hulbert's five years as League president was his total opposition to seeking new teams from New York and Philadelphia to play in the League. It had been Hulbert's contention when he first offered his plan for the National League back in '75 that all the problems of the old National Association — meaning drinking and gambling — were rooted in New York and Philadelphia. Then when the Athletics and Mutuals folded in the final month of the National League's initial season, Hulbert became convinced that teams in those two cities would be constant sources of problems for the League. Even when the Louisville gambling scandal of '77 was exposed, Hulbert pointed up how all of the men involved in the crime had direct connections with New York or Philadelphia or both at one time or another. The National League's ability to survive and actually thrive without the two eastern metropolises only served to reinforce Hulbert's adamant stand.

At the winter meetings of '82, Abraham G. Mills, a Washington attorney with connections to Chicago and a part owner in the Chicago Ball Club, was elected president of the National League. Mills was as forceful in personality as Hulbert had been, but he was more intellectually astute than the deceased founder of the League and less prejudiced when it came to business. Mills had no problems with having Philadelphia and New York in the National League again.

All through the year, Mills and the other NL magnates were convinced that Jim Mutrie's New York Metropolitans would join the League for the '83 season. Much to their surprise, Mutrie opted for the American Association instead. To replace the Mets, John B. Day's New York club was voted into the League with a new nine from Philadelphia. With the Mets and a Columbus, Ohio team joining the AA, both loops now had eight teams.

At this time, the Northwest League returned to life at a meeting of representatives from eight cities at Fort Wayne, Indiana. The Northwest League magnates feared that the warring NL and AA would sign away their best players. To prevent any such destructive moves by the big city circuits, the Northwest League leaders approached Mills and asked for an agreement to be reached that would protect them from predatory raids by the NL.

Mills wisely seized the opportunity and invited the AA to join in a peace conference with the new league's delegates. At this meeting, a new *National Agreement*, known initially as the *Tri–Partite Pact*, was drawn up and accepted by the National and Northwest Leagues. The AA only agreed to sign the document after much heated discussion a few weeks later, and even then, many of the Association's magnates had their doubts about the treaty because of the reserve clause it contained whereby each team was entitled to place 11 players on its reserve list from season to season.

The Tri–Partite Pact marked the beginning of *Organized Baseball* in the United States.

Now that peace was restored to the baseball world the teams got down to the business of playing the game on the field.

The White Stockings had almost the same team as they had in '82. The only major change in the roster was the release of Joe Quest, who signed on with Detroit, and the signing of Fred Pfeffer, who had played for the defunct Troy team in '82. Silver Flint was still the number one catcher; Cap Anson on first; Tommy Burns at short; Ned Williamson at third; Abner Dalrymple in left; George Gore in center; and the inimitable King Kelly in right. Larry Corcoran and Fred Goldsmith still made up the pitching staff, and Goldsmith also played right when Kelly was behind the plate.

With two new teams in the League, formerly weak nines like Detroit, Cleveland, and Buffalo figured to finish higher and possibly challenge for the pennant. Even so, the White Stockings were favored to repeat as National League champions. Boston and Providence were given only fair chances to overtake Chicago in '83. New York and Philadelphia weren't even considered in the oddsmaking.

The Whites got off to a typical start, sweeping three straight from Detroit in Michigan. They opened their home season on May 5, 1883 by showing off their new uniforms: red caps, white shirts, and red knickers. Of course, they still wore the now traditional white stockings. The new duds didn't help them win though.

Late in May Anson hired a new substitute outfielder, a young man from Ames, Iowa named Billy Sunday. The newcomer wasn't much with the stick, but he could run, catch, and throw with the best of them.

After a month of playing, the White Stockings led the League with a 16–7 record to Cleveland's 14–7 and 13–9 for Detroit and Providence. On June 9, the four-team race had Cleveland in first by percentage points but the Whites in first on wins, which counted more in '83 than percentage of victories did. By June 16, Providence had catapulted over both western nines to take over first, and Boston had surpassed Detroit to inhabit fourth place behind Cleveland and Chicago. The White Stockings hit their low point of the season a week later when their record bottomed out at 19–17 and they had slipped to fourth, eight wins behind League–leading Providence.

The White Stockings faced Buffalo on July 3, but the Bison should have stayed home. Anson and Dalrymple each had four doubles during the contest; and Anson, Dalrymple, and Kelly each had five hits with Gore and Williamson adding four each. For the game, the Whites pounded out a total of 32 hits, including 14 two–baggers. The final score was 31–7. Unfortunately, this was only one game, not a whole season.

The Providence Grays continued to lead the National League into the first week of July with 33 wins to Cleveland's 30, Boston's 28, and Chicago's 26. The Cleveland Spiders took over first place for a day the following week with a 35–15 mark to Providence's 35–19 record. Boston was still five wins back, but the White Stockings had gained a game. On the last Sunday of the month, Providence was again in first at 41–20, Cleveland in second at 39–19, and the Whites had climed back into third at 35–23.

It was at this time that A.H. Soden replaced Jack Burdock with John Morrill as captain of the Boston Reds.

As the '83 season moved into August, the NL race turned into a five–team affair. Providence still had the most wins, 41, with Cleveland only one behind at 40, Chicago three back at 38, Boston at 36, and Buffalo suddenly coming on at 33.

On the final weekend of the month, the chase for the

flag was closer than ever. Cleveland regained the top with 48 wins, Providence 47, Chicago 45, Boston 44, and Buffalo 41. With a full five weeks of play to go, any of these five teams could still take the title.

The National League pennant fight got as tight as it ever would get in any year on September 1. Cleveland and Providence were tied with 49 wins each, and Boston and the White Stockings were only one win back at 48 each. This was the most pivotal part of the year for the Chicagoans because they were beginning their final home stand and would be playing their last 13 games on the road.

Anson's gang peaked a little early on September 6 against Detroit. On that day, they scored 26 runs, 18 of them in the seventh inning. Tommy Burns had the best day of his career when he hit three doubles and a homer. Chicago moved into first place with the 26–6 mauling of the Michigan nine.

The White Stockings couldn't stay in first place for more than five days because they had become a little complacent and the Boston Reds seemed to be more inspired to win. On September 11, the Beantown boys slipped into the top slot ahead of both Chicago and Providence in second. The Whites lost four straight to slip all the way to fourth by September 15, then nipped Providence, 8–7, in Rhode Island to break the skein. In the meantime, Boston kept on winning. Buffalo was eliminated on the 19th, leaving only four teams in the race.

With only a week left in the campaign, Boston and Providence had 57 wins each, but Providence had two more losses than the Reds with 37. The Whites were 55–39, and Cleveland was 54–38.

Boston had already won 13 of 16 games, including four

wins over the White Stockings in Beantown. Chicago won its final four games, but it availed the Whites nothing as the Reds took all six of their remaining contests to win the pennant going away. John Morrill kicked his team to the pennant by going 32–9 over the final two months of the campaign.

The big reason for the White Stockings fall from the top was Mike Kelly's drinking. The King had his worst season ever in a Chicago uniform, hitting only .255 and slugging a mere .388. With Kelly's performance off, the whole team was affected. Anson hit only .308, which was a bad year for him.

The National League and the American Association had disagreed on various points in '82, especially about selling beer at the ball park and playing games on Sundays; but they didn't conduct massive player raids on each other because their leaders had considered how disastrous the consequences of such action could be. Then the Northwest League forged a peace between the two major leagues in early '83, although that was hardly the minor loop's intent. For most of the year, harmony reigned over the baseball world. However, dark clouds were on the horizon.

A new movement was afoot in baseball, led by Henry V. Lucas, scion of a wealthy old St. Louis family and possessor of a considerable fortune stemming from his grandfather, an early settler of St. Louis, who had purchased large tracts of land in and around the city. Henry's brother, John B.C. Lucas, was president of the St. Louis Base Ball Association in the 1870s and of the National League club located there in '77. Henry Lucas had a team, and he wanted to get it into one of the two major leagues, preferably the AA. Problem was the AA already had a team in St. Louis, the Browns. Problem with joining the NL, if they would have him, was the very things that separated the two circuits in the first place: 50-cent admissions, no beer, and no Sunday games.

Lucas wasn't the only magnate with problems like these. Owners of independent teams in several other cities were faced with the same dilemma. A.H. Henderson, a Baltimore mattress manufacturer, made a substantial investment in a team in his own city, then put up the money for a nine in Chicago that was established on June 6, 1883. These two teams played each other frequently that year, and they also played independents from Washington, Pittsburgh, and Altoona, Pennsylvania as well as Lucas' St. Louis club. They had no formal organization but designated themselves the Union Association.

Lucas, Henderson, and the other magnates felt the reserve clause was "the most arbitrary and unjust rule ever suggested" and that "it ought to be broken." With this purpose in mind, the independents met in Pittsburgh on September 12, 1883 and drew up a constitution and by-laws for a legal entity that would be known as the Union Association. From that point forward, all out war was declared between Organized Baseball (the National League, American Association, and Northwest League) and the Union forces. The Unions encouraged Tri-Partite players to jump their contracts and sign with the team of their choice in the UA. Some 30 of them did, but few of these actually played for Union teams. Larry Corcoran of the White Stockings was one of these to jump over the fence, then jump back before the actual playing season began. None of his teammates took advantage of the Unions' generosity, every one of them stating simply that they were happy where they were.

Bury My Heart at Wrigley Field

The Unions did have a big effect on the two established organizations in that they caused the formation of a *reserve league*. In order to deprive the UA of players and to have a ready supply of talent should any regular player become injured or ill during the season, each of the NL and AA clubs hired a complete roster of reserve players. These teams practiced with the regulars in the spring, then played other reserve teams once the season began. The reserve league was the forerunner to the minor league system of later years.

Some of the reserve players did jump their contracts and play for UA teams, and some of them went on to play in the NL and AA. Of the White Stockings' reserves, Bernie Graham played for the Chicago and Baltimore entries in the UA; Sam King hustled for Washington of the AA; Tom McDermott played for Baltimore of the AA; Gurdon Whiteley played for Boston and Cleveland in the NL; George Crosby pitched in three games for the White Stockings; and Walt Kinzie got into 19 games for the Whites and 11 for St. Louis of the AA. One of the Chicago *Tribune* writers called the youngsters on the reserve team "the Colts". This was the very first instance of a writer using this term in reference to a Chicago team.

The White Stockings opened their '84 season in New York in front of a full house that thoroughly enjoyed watching their "Giants" maul the Whites, 15–3. New Yorkers continued to delight in their team's performance over the next two days as Chicago fell twice more. After 10 days of play, the Whites were in fourth place with a 3–4 record.

Chicago's road trip continued for the whole month of May.

When the Whites reached home on June 1, 1884, they

were mired in fifth place at 9–15, a full 11 games behind frontrunner Providence. The Grays' former manager, Harry Wright, had moved on to Philadelphia to manage the new team there; and Frank Bancroft, the former manager of Worcester ('80), Detroit ('81–'82), and Cleveland ('83) nines had assumed the reins of leadership. Bancroft had the Grays off to an incredible start at 20–4, but it must be remembered that all of their games were played at home that first month.

None of the Chicago players got off to a particularly good start in '84, and they didn't get much better as spring turned into summer. The Whites finally reached the .500–mark on July 12 when they downed Detroit, 6–5, but they couldn't get over the break even point or just stay there. Anson and Spalding tried everything to improve the team's performance, but neither Anson's screamed threats nor Spalding's shuffling of players on and off the roster helped. The White Stockings were simply having a bad year that had its roots in a policy that Anson established before spring practice even began.

Mike Kelly was well known around the League cities as a heavy drinker and real lady–killer. He was a big, handsome Irishman who had a line of good–natured, harmless malarkey that endeared him to everyone who came in contact with him, men as well as the more beautiful single ladies who worked the saloons and restaurants that Kelly visited on the road and habituated in Chicago. Kelly was also the leader of a whole group of single players who caroused to the wee hours while the team was on the road.

Anson wasn't among this clique because he was married and because he didn't go in for that sort of entertainment. He didn't exactly hold with his players' behavior off the field, but he would have been the first to defend their right to enjoy themselves as they wished — until such behavior affected their play on the field. It was his feeling that the White Stockings had barely won the pennant in '82 and then lost it in '83 because of Kelly's late night activities. To prevent another second place finish and to put the Whites back on top of the League, Anson instituted a curfew of 11:00 p.m. for the players when the team was on the road.

Kelly and his little band of merrymakers resented Anson's new rule, and they voiced their displeasure openly in the press, stating they were gentlemen entitled to their leisure after a hard day on the playing field; they weren't school boys who needed their nightly rest in order to stay awake in the classroom. Some of them threatened to jump to the UA, but Anson wouldn't back down; the curfew was there to stay.

The White Stockings climbed back over the .500–mark in mid–August only to fall four games under again two weeks later at 41–45. On September 4, Chicago was eliminated from the pennant race, but the season was hardly over.

With the team playing poorly, attendance dropped off slightly for the Chicago Ball Club. Always the "Scrooge" type, Spalding thought to save money by releasing Fred Goldsmith and hiring Joe Brown from the disbanded Ft. Wayne team of the Northwest League to replace him. Brown finished the season, going 4–2, but was gone the next year.

One man that Spalding hired that summer of '84 who did stick around a while was a 23–years–old Cambridge, Massachusetts native named John Gibson Clarkson, a righthanded flame thrower who had played briefly with Worcester in '82. In '83, he played for Saginaw, Michigan of the Northwest League. Anson spotted him in a non–league game in late August of '84 and urged Spalding to give the youngster a contract. Clarkson was one bright spot in a dismal season as he won 10 and lost only three in the latter part of the campaign.

The White Stockings finished a distant fourth at 62–50, 22 games behind pennant–winning Providence. Larry Corcoran won 35 but lost 23; Goldsmith was 9–11; and an aggregate of others were 4–11. Corcoran also pitched his third no–hitter in a Chicago uniform on June 27. Anson's curfew had a telling effect on Kelly as the King won the batting title with a .354 mark. Anson hit .335; Gore, .319; and Dalrymple, .309. These numbers were normal, nothing out of the usual for any team or any group of players of their time. But some of the Chicago players did have statistics that were odd actually; maybe even downright freakish.

When the new Lakefront Park was built between Randolph and Washington streets and Michigan Avenue and the lake in '77, the playing field was laid out strangely. The park was rectangular in shape, which was nothing unusual because all baseball parks were either square or rectangular in those days; but most other parks had their playing fields laid out with the home plate point of the diamond in the middle of one *end* of the rect-angular park or in the middle of one *side* of the square park.

At Lakefront Park, home plate was placed in one *corner* of the rectangular park, creating an odd config-uration for the playing field giving it a very short right field fence.*

* The distance down the right field foul line has been estimated by some historians to have been as short as 230 feet and as long as 275 feet. More than likely it was

Bury My Heart at Wrigley Field

The White Stockings led the National League in hitting doubles from 1879–83, but they were consistently on the lower end of the scale in triples and homers. That all changed with the new ground rule.

In all the years before '84, a ball hit over a certain section of the right field fence was considered to be a ground rule double. For '84, someone thought it would be great if the ground rule was changed to allow any ball hit over any portion of the outfield fence to be a home run.

The fun started with the very first home game of the season for the White Stockings on May 29. Abner Dalrymple led off and clubbed a liner over the right field fence off Detroit's George Weidman. Then Detroit's first hitter banged one out in the same area in the bottom half of the frame. When the game was over a total of five

somewhere in between, most likely about 250 feet. If the 230 feet mark is accepted, then dead right field would be 257 feet and dead center would be 325 feet. If the 275 feet distance is accepted, then dead right would be 307 feet and dead center 389 feet. If a 250 feet distance is accepted, then dead right becomes 280 feet and dead center 354 feet. In parks that had normal foul line distances of over 300 feet with dead right and dead left around 350 feet and dead center close to 400 feet, heavy hitters were still reaching the fences on occasion. Even in Chicago, an occasional homer was hit over the left field fence which was 350 away. Although this was the era of the dead ball, the former set of figures seems to be absolutely ludicrous and the latter doesn't appear to jive with the known facts. Therefore, this author is inclined to think that the middle set of numbers is most likely correct.

homers had been hit; a very unusual total for that era.

The very next day Ned Williamson made history when he socked three round–trippers in the nightcap of a Memorial Day morning–afternoon doubleheader.

In the first five games of the season in Chicago, 25 homers were hit by the White Stockings and their visitors. By season's end, a whopping total of 197 four-baggers were pounded out of Lakefront Park, 130 by the White Stockings. Williamson set a record with 27 homers, a mark that would hold up for 35 years until Babe Ruth came along. Close behind the Chicago third-baseman were Fred Pfeffer with 25, Dalrymple with 22, and Anson with 21. As a team, the White Stockings hit 142 homers, a mark that would stand up well into the next century.

The greatest feat of the season belonged to Anson. On August 5, he punched two balls over the short field fence, then topped that by hitting three out the next day, giving him a two–day total of five round–trippers. This feat was not to be duplicated until the immortal Ty Cobb accomplished it on May 5–6, 1925.

The close of the '84 season was also the swan song for the ill–fated Union Association. Before the playing campaign was a month old over some of its teams had either folded or moved to other cities. Only a handful of its clubs played a complete schedule, if it could be called a schedule.

The cause of the demise of the UA lay directly at the feet of the very men who supported it. Although they had the money to operate the organization for several years, they squandered it all that first campaign through mismanagement and a basic ignorance of professional sports. Their only achievements were the solidification of the two established major leagues and the confirmation that the Tri–Partite Pact was the only way for new leagues to go if they wished to be successful. In short, the failure of the Union Association put Organized Baseball on terra firma — for good!

15

New Park, New Flag

Henry Lucas did accomplish one thing with his Union Association: he got a team in the National League for '85.

The Cleveland Spiders were only NL casualty of the baseball war, and Lucas' St. Louis Reds — about the only survivor of the UA — were admitted to replace the Ohio club.

The Chicago Ball Club came out of the conflict un-scathed. The entire team was intact. Cap Anson was back, of course, for his 10th season as a player and seventh as field boss. Fred Pfeffer, the Louisville native, returned to play second base for the third year in a row for the White Stockings. Tommy Burns would be at shortstop; Ned Williamson at third; Abner Dalrymple in left field; George Gore in center; Mike Kelly in right; and Silver Flint behind the plate. This latter group was beginning their sixth consecutive campaign in Chicago. For a pitching staff, Anson had Larry Corcoran, John Clarkson, and Joe Brown. On the bench were Billy Sunday, Sy Sutcliffe, Nat Kellogg, Ollie Beard, and Fred Mann.

Spalding put his players in new uniforms and a new ball park that spring. He dressed them in knit jerseys of navy blue trimmed with white collars and cuffs, navy blue pants, white belts, white caps, and, of course, white stockings. The new playing field was being built on the West Side in an area bounded on the south by Harrison Street, on the north by Congress Street, on the east by Throop, and on the west by Loomis.

Anson packed up the boys in early April and took them south for a series of exhibition games. They started off by playing in Louisville and Cincinnati against the American Association teams of those cities, then continued on south to play Nashville, Chattanooga, and Atlanta of the Southern League. When the team returned to Chicago for the opening of the '85 campaign, Brown, Kellogg, Beard, and Mann were all released, and the remainder of the squad took a temperance pledge.

The '85 campaign began inauspiciously enough. The new St. Louis franchise nipped the White Stockings, 3–1, in the Mound City. Then Chicago reeled off four straight wins before bowing to the New York Giants on an eastern road trip. After three more wins, the Whites dropped another one to New York, and 17 days into the season, Chicago stood second at 7–4 to the Giants' 9–2.

Unlike many other years where two teams get off to a good start then fade into the pack later on, Chicago and New York remained on top of the heap throughout the year.

During the following week, Clarkson shut out Providence on successive days, 10–0 and 2–0, to extend a Chicago winning streak to four games; then he whitewashed Boston, 1–0, two days later. His string of goose eggs came to a halt in Boston two days after that when he beat the Braves, 6–1, stretching the win skein to seven games before the Beantowners ended it the next day.

West Side Grounds was almost completed by the end

of May. All that remained was the completion of the construction of a 12–foot brick wall around the new park. To finance this project, Al Spalding induced the club's minority stockholders to buy up a new issue of stock. The wall was finished by the first week in June.

The White Stockings continued their long road trip into the first few days of June. They swept four straight in Detroit, then headed home with an outstanding record of 18–6, still trailing the Giants at 19–5.

Appropriately, the first visitor to West Side Grounds was the St. Louis club of Henry Lucas. Clarkson took the mound for the Whites and beat the Reds, 9–2. Chicago continued its winning ways by sweeping St. Louis, extending their winning streak to eight games, and capturing the top spot in the National League for the first time in '85. The Giants joined the White Stockings atop the standings the next day, but the tie didn't last as Chicago continued its winning ways and New York lost twice.

Philadelphia's Ed Daily finally stopped the Whites, 2–0, in Chicago on June 25. The loss set Chicago's home record at 14–1 and at 32–7 overall. After another loss and a win, the White Stockings stood two victories ahead of New York, eight ahead of third place Providence, and 13 ahead of the Phillies in fourth. The first week of July featured a show down series between the White Stock- ings and the Giants in Chicago, including a July 4th morning–afternoon twinbill. Two big crowds — 11,000 in the a.m. and 9,000 in the p.m. – showed up at West Side Grounds to greet the New Yorkers on Indepen- dence Day. The Giants took the opener, 6–3, but the Whites salvaged a split by winning the nightcap by the same score. The other games in the series were also divided by the two contenders, leaving the race tightly contested with the White Stockings in first at 37–10 and the Giants in second at 35–11.

With the season nearly half over, Billy Sunday was hitting .371 as a substitute outfielder and George Gore was leading the NL in homers with five. No other Chicago player was hitting over .300 or among the leaders in any offensive statistical category. The secret to the Whites' success was the iron man performance of John Clarkson. The National League's top hurler's record stood at an incredible 28–6 on the morning of July 5. This would have been an impressive mark for a full season, even in the 1880s; but the White Stockings still had 65 games to play. The question remained: Could Clarkson hold up through the whole season?

On July 9, Gore collected three doubles and two triples in an 8–5 win over Providence. It was only one of two wins for the White Stockings that week. They lost three, while New York was winning three and losing twice to close the gap between them to a half game. The following week the Whites swept a five–game series at Buffalo, then beat Boston for a sixth straight win. New York managed to win four but lost twice, giving the White Stockings some breathing room.

The big news of the month was the release of Larry Corcoran and the signing of the porky Scot, Jim McCormick, the pitcher who could be as tough as any moundsman — when he was sober. Corcoran was let go because his arm was worn out, but Corcoran denied that his arm was injured. Later in the season, he was able to convince the Giants' manager, Jim Mutrie, that he was okay and he signed a contract with New York. He won two and lost one in three appearances for the Giants. McCormick had started the '85 season with Providence but was released because the Grays had difficulty meeting his salary and because of his drinking habits. Frank Bancroft claimed the latter, and McCormick said it was the former. It was actually a combination of both reasons.

Whatever the reason for McCormick's release, Spalding didn't care. Anson needed another arm to support Clarkson if the White Stockings were going to win another pennant, and McCormick was the best man available.

Jim McCormick began his NL career with Indianapolis in '78, then moved to Cleveland when the Indiana club folded. In five–plus seasons with the Spiders, McCormick won 173 games and lost 162. He jumped to the Union Association in '84 and posted 21–3 record in a partial season with the Cincinnati club.

The White Stockings were 45–13 when McCormick joined the team on July 20. Two weeks later their record was 53–15, and New York was a game and a half back. Providence was a distant third at 40–24, 11 games behind. For all practical purposes, the other five teams were out of the race by August 1. Providence was able to last into the first week of September before being eliminated, leaving the White Stockings and Giants to fight it out for first.

On September 19, the White Stockings managed to build a three–game lead over the Giants, but the pennant race wasn't the big news of the day.

The Buffalo club was not having a good year, either on the field or at the box office. In order to survive to the end of the season and pay off a few pressing debts, the Buffalo managers decided to sell the club to the Detroit club's owners. The new owners of the Buffalo club then decided to "transfer" Buffalo's four best players — Dan Brouthers, Hardy Richardson, Jack Rowe, and Deacon

White — to Detroit to play out the remainder of the season, leaving Buffalo with a makeshift nine to finish the schedule.

Protests rose from every corner; not so much out of worry about the outcome of the '85 season but from concern about the coming year of '86. Detroit was well out of the '85 race. The four star players might help them win a lot of games in the final month of play but not enough to prevent either Chicago or New York from winning the pennant. No, it was the transaction of "moving" the players from one team to another without them being released, and thus made available to the other League teams, that bothered everyone.

NL President Nick Young ruled that the four players in question were still the property of the Buffalo franchise, no matter who owned that franchise. The only way the players could change teams was to go through the released player process or to be left unreserved at the end of the season and sign new contracts with the team of their choice. The latter option was exactly what the Detroit–Buffalo owners chose to do later that fall, and Brouthers, Richardson, Rowe, and White joined the Detroit nine for '86.

Once the dispute over "The Big Four" was concluded the baseball world turned its focus back to the pennant race in the National League.

The Giants clipped a game off Chicago's lead during the fourth week of September, but the magic number of White Stockings wins and New York losses for the Whites to win the pennant was down to seven. The Giants were due into Chicago for one final series of four games that would either make or break the pennant hopes of the New Yorkers.

Advance ticket sales for the first game of the series

were the strongest they had ever been in Chicago. League President Nick Young and the presidents of several other clubs planned to be in attendance. Jim McCormick, who was in the midst of a 14–game winning streak, was slated to take the mound for the White Stockings. White Stocking Park was packed to the rafters when the umpire called out for the players to "play ball!" McCormick wasn't at his best, but he was good enough to win, 7–4. The victory lowered Chicago's magic number to five.

The next morning, September 30, 1885, the Chicago White Stockings made front page news in the Chicago *Tribune* for the first time in their history.

Clarkson stepped into the pitcher's box for the second game. He pitched better than McCormick did the day before, but didn't get the same support. Even so, Fred Pfeffer's solo homer over the right field wall was enough of a difference in the 2–1 game. The White Stockings lowered their magic number to three, and the Giants pennant hopes began to look bleak.

McCormick repeated his performance of two days earlier on October 1, and the hitters did their part as the Whites whipped the Giants for the third straight day, 8–3. Chicago was bedlam that late afternoon and evening as everyone realized that the White Stockings had clinched a tie for the pennant, and all their team had to do was win one more game or the New Yorkers lose one more to make the Whites NL champs for '85.

The Giants delayed any pennant–winning celebrations when they pounded Clarkson, 13–8, on October 3. The whole baseball world knew the setback was only temporary; the White Stockings had a lock on the flag and that was that.

McCormick continued his winning ways on October 6

when he bested the Phillies, 9–4, to give the White Stockings the title. Tommy Burns did his part by slugging a pair of homers over the distant left field wall.* With the pennant tucked neatly away in their pockets, the White Stockings dropped the final three games of the series but did finish two games ahead of New York.

In '82, Al Spalding had arranged a post–season series for his NL champion White Stockings with the Cincinnati Reds, winners of the American Association's first pennant. The two teams played a pair of contests, then were forced to halt the series when AA President Denny McKnight threatened to expel the Cincinnati club. If not for McKnight's stand against playing NL clubs, this would have been the first World Series.

In '83, the Philadelphia Athletics and Boston Braves set up a post–season series but never played it. The A's played a few other NL teams first and did very poorly. In order to prevent further embarrassment, the Philadelphia management called off the games with Boston.

The first World Series was finally played in '84 when the Providence Grays and New York Mets went head-to-head for a mythical claim to the best team in the world. Charles "Hoss" Radbourne, who had pitched an incredible 679 innings and had won 60 games during the regular season, mowed down the Mets in three straight to give the Grays bragging rights.

For '85, Spalding and Chris Von Der Ahe, the owner of the St. Louis Browns, began corresponding with each other about a possible post–season series. The Browns wrapped up their title early in September, and once the

---

* The newspapers didn't say whether the wind was blowing out that day, but for Burns to hit a pair over the leftfield wall, it had to be.

White Stockings did likewise in October, Spalding and Von Der Ahe finalized the arrangements for their teams to play. For incentive, the owners offered the winning team $1,000. Actually, the losing team had to *pay* the winner the grand, which made the *offer a bet* in reality.

Fred Pfeffer hit a homer in the 8th inning to tie up the first game at 5–5. Then the contest was called on account of darkness, making the result a tie.

Game 2 was forfeited to the White Stockings when St. Louis captain Charles Comiskey pulled his team off the field when he disagreed with an umpire's decision.

The Browns won the third game, 7–4, and they won the fourth game, 3–2.

Games 5 and 6 were taken by Chicago by the identical scores of 9–2.

St. Louis won the seventh contest in the series, 13–4, evening the series at three wins, three losses, and a tie for each team. There was talk about playing a tie–breaker, but nothing came of it, leaving the outcome of the playoff undecided. The baseball world would have no undisputed champion for 1885.

16

Swan Song for a Dynasty

All good things must come to an end — or so it seems.

Once again the National League magnates hit a snag at their winter meetings in '85. In fact, they hit several.

The Providence Grays were dropped from the League because their management couldn't make good on the monetary guarantee required by NL rules for the coming season. Without absolute assurance that a team could complete its schedule, a club was denied membership in the League.

The Detroit owners who bought out the Buffalo Bisons club in September decided against fielding a team in the upstate New York city for the '86 campaign, which left another hole in the League. The NL magnates offered Providence's spot to Charles H. Byrne, the owner of the Brooklyn club in the American Association. Byrne was delighted to join but on one condition. He wanted first choice of the Providence players who were now free agents because their team had folded. The Philadelphia and Boston clubs objected, denying Byrne the three-fourths vote needed for approval, so the Brooklyn mogul said he'd stay in the AA for '86.

This delighted the AA owners exceedingly, but Spalding and the other NL leaders didn't lose any sleep over the fact that their loop had only six teams in it over the winter of 1885-86.

With the coming of the new year, NL President Nicholas Young decided something had to be done to give the League a full complement of teams. He called a meeting for mid-January 1886 to take up this very question. The magnates accepted the application of the Washington club for a franchise, and the Senators joined the National League as the replacement for Providence.

This put four teams in the East but left only three in the West. Because of the owners' desire for geographical balance, Buffalo, having been considered a western team, would have to be replaced by another western city. The candidates were Indianapolis, Milwaukee, and Kansas City. Both Milwaukee and Indianapolis had been in the NL in '78. Indianapolis had been in the American Association in '84, and Milwaukee had been briefly represented in the Union Association the same year. Kansas City had supported a minor league team for a few years and had been in the UA. The convention couldn't reach a decision in January, so the meeting was adjourned without an eighth team being admitted to the NL. Pres. Young took a poll by mail in early February, and Kansas City was voted into the circuit.

More and more it was becoming evident to baseball managers that two pitchers couldn't carry a team for a whole season, not when the schedule called for 112 games. The White Stockings had been lucky to get through the '85 season with John Clarkson carrying the load until Jim McCormick joined the team to give him some needed rest for the pennant drive.

For '86, Anson knew that at least three good men would be needed for mound duty, especially since the schedule had been increased to 126 games and because the Detroit Wolverines had loaded their team with Dan Brouthers, Deacon White, Hardy Richardson, and Jack Rowe. Anse had McCormick and Clarkson back in the fold already, and in early March he signed John "Jocko" Flynn, a fireballing lefty from Lawrence, Massachusetts. Cap also hired Flynn's batterymate and home town buddy George "Prunes" Moolic as a third regular catcher.

The rest of the roster looked the same as it had for most of the decade to date. Silver Flint was again behind the plate; Anson on first; Pfeffer on second; Abner Dalrymple in left; George Gore in center; King Kelly in right and also slated to catch. Ned Williamson and Tommy Burns were also back, but Anson switched them around in the field, moving Williamson to short and Burns to third. Backing up just about everyone would be a hot-headed young Irishman, James E. Ryan, who had been signed the year before for the last few games of the season.

With his team intact by March 15, Anson took his players to Hot Springs, Arkansas to "boil off their winter fat" and prepare them for the coming campaign. This was the first time the White Stockings had gone south for spring training since being a member of the National League. Joining them for a short while was the Chicago *Tribune*'s sports editor, Harry Palmer. After a few weeks of sweating it out in the baths, on the training table, and in the field, the Whites started playing exhibitions against Southern League and Texas League teams as well as a few other NL opponents and AA nines. By the end of April, they were ready to begin the defense of their crown.

The Kansas City Cowboys were given the privilege of hosting the Whites for the opening of the '86 season, and the KC boys proved to be rather rude, forcing the game to go 13 innings before finally succumbing, 6–5. Clarkson did his iron man act, going the distance for the victory.

Clarkson won his next start in St. Louis, downing the Maroons, 7–3; then lost his first game the day after. He won Chicago's home opener, beating Detroit, 5–1, on May 6; then lost the next two. By the end of the month, the Wolverines were on top of the League standings with a 21–5 mark, while the White Stockings were 19–5, all five losses being charged to Clarkson.

Because the rules still stated that a player couldn't be substituted for unless he was injured or ill, a relief pitcher had to be in the game from the start. Anson had used King Kelly, Fred Pfeffer, and Ned Williamson as change pitchers in the past when one of the other pitchers wasn't playing in the outfield. Each one had been adequate, but none was a threat to break into the starting rotation. The captain had even taken a turn in the pitcher's box himself on a couple of occasions. So based on past experience, Anse gave Jimmy Ryan a shot at change pitching in a game in late May. Ryan acquitted himself satisfactorily, and the Whites had another weapon to add to their arsenal.

In early June, Tommy Burns pulled one of those boners that make baseball so interesting and unique as a kids game being played by grown men who often act like children, especially at salary time. The Whites were playing the New York Giants in Chicago. It was the top of the ninth, and the score was tied at seven apiece. Anson was on third, and Pfeffer was perched on second with two out. Burns lined a single to center, and both runners made for the plate and arrived safely. Thinking it was the *bottom* of the ninth, Burns turned away from the basepath before reaching first and headed for the club-house. The alert Giants' first-sacker, Roger Connor, called for the ball from outfielder Orator Jim O'Rourke, got it, and tagged the bag. The umpire called Burns out, nullifying both runs,* and the game continued. New York failed to score in their half of the frame, and the game was called because of darkness, ending in a tie.

Detroit continued to lead the League through the middle of June, having a perfect home record until the White Stockings visited the Michigan city. Then on the 19th Chicago upended the Wolverines, 5–4, which only closed the gap between the two teams to a game and a half. Detroit won the next one to put the White Stockings back to two and a half behind.

The Giants and the Phillies were slowly creeping up on the two leaders, and both teams were ready to gain even more ground when the Wolverines called on the White Stockings during the second week of July for a three-game set. Chicago was four and a half games behind when the series began and only one and a half back when Detroit left town three days later.

For the next three weeks, the Whites matched the Wolverines win for win until they ran into a buzzsaw in New York. The Giants whipped Chicago three straight and moved to within two games of second, while the White Stockings fell to three and a half back of Detroit.

The picture looked bleak for Anson's gang in early August because Pfeffer, Williamson, and Gore went down with injuries. Anson was so desperate for help that

* This incident is not to be confused with the Fred Merkle incident of two decades later, which oddly enough involved the same two teams only the result was just the opposite for the Cubs.

he had Ryan playing second and Jocko Flynn was at short for what might have been the only lefthanded doubleplay combination in the history of the game.

Fortunately, the Giants weren't a team to play favorites. After working over the Whites, they did the same to Detroit, tightening the race even further. New York now trailed Chicago by one and a half and Detroit by two and a half. The White Stockings were only a pair of wins behind the Wolverines. Just for spice, the Phillies were on a rampage and had moved to within nine and a half games of first place on August 11.

About this time, the St. Louis Maroons appeared to be in the throes of death as Henry Lucas refused to spend any more money on his club. The team played like it was already dead, and rumors circulated through the baseball world that Pittsburgh would be replacing St. Louis in '87.

Detroit took advantage of the St. Louis situation and the incompetence of the Washington and Kansas City nines and once again built up a lead of five games over the Giants and 12½ over Philadelphia. Unfortunately for the Wolverines, the Whites were just as capable of mistreating the Missouri teams and Washington, and Chicago closed to a half game of the League's leaders on August 25. The next day the White Stockings pounded on Boston, 10–4, as Kelly and a healthy Ned Williamson homered in support of Clarkson who was coming on again as the team's top hurler. At the same time, the Phillies outslugged Detroit, 11–10, to put Chicago on top of the League standings for the first time since the opening days of the '86 season.

The Whites put a little breathing room between themselves and Detroit the following afternoon when Flynn nailed down Philadelphia, 13–1, from the pitcher's box and the plate as he also hit a home run; and Boston was beating the Wolverines, 7–3.

By September 8, the White Stockings had won 12 straight and built a three–game lead over their Michigan rivals. Philadelphia was fading from the race, and the Giants were barely holding their own, now 14 games back. The 12th win in the skein was the end of a three–game sweep of New York as Kelly pounded out a four–bagger behind Flynn's tough twirling. It appeared that Anson had finally found the winning combination by having Ryan in left in place of the slumping Dalrymple during the entire streak.

The Wolverines invaded Chicago for a three–game showdown series on September 9. Detroit captured the first game, 8–3, to bring an end to the Whites' winning string, but Chicago won the next day, 14–8, in spite of Dan Brouthers' three homers, double, and single. With a 14–4 win of the third game, the White Stockings sent the Wolverines packing four games back. By the end of the week, Chicago's magic number of wins and Detroit losses was down to 19.

The White Stockings swept a four–game series from the Cowboys in Kansas City, while the Wolverines were doing the same to the Maroons in St. Louis. Then it was time for another showdown series between the two leaders, but this time in Detroit.

With their magic number now at 15, the Whites nailed down the first game of the Detroit series by scoring four runs in the first inning, then holding on to win, 7–3, behind Clarkson. The win reduced their magic number to 13 and put Chicago five and a half games up on Detroit. The pressure was really on the Wolverines now. They had to win or face an uphill battle that they were almost sure to lose. Their fans realized this all too well when the two League foes squared off for the second game in the series.

Because the League wanted to accommodate the working fans, games were usually scheduled to start at 3:30 p.m., then were played to their conclusion or darkness, depending on which came first. In the later months of the season, few games were ever played to their full nine innings. The length of most games was determined by cloud conditions. The cloudier the day, the sooner the umpire called a halt to the game, even if it meant the game would end in a tie.

Weather conditions weren't ideal for the second game in the Detroit–Chicago set. It had been threatening to rain all day, but the home team decided to try playing the game anyway. After four innings, played mostly in a steady drizzle, Umpire Powers called the contest off, which pleased the Detroit kranks because the White Stockings were ahead. This meant the game would have to be replayed entirely.

The next day the skies threatened again, but the moisture held off. Detroit batted first and took an early lead. The Whites stormed back, and by the top of the seventh, Chicago led, 6–3. Detroit came to bat under darkening clouds and scored once on a homer by big Dan Brouthers to close the gap to 6–4. The Whites came to bat in the bottom of the frame and started another rally.

Gore and Kelly walked and were followed by a hit by Anson. Both runners scored, and Anson went to second on the throw home. He advanced to third on Pfeffer's ground out, then came across the plate on a hit by Burns. The Chicago thirdbaseman tried to reach second on the play, and a good throw, catch, and tag by the Detroit defenders made it a close call for the umpire. Powers ruled Burns safe, and a roar of disapproval shook the stands. After another out and a double by Hardie that brought in Burns, making the score, 10–4, Powers gazed heavenward, then stepped up to the plate and announced to the crowd that the game was over, that he was calling it due to darkness.

Thinking little more of his decision and disregarding the hissing and catcalling from the Detroit partisans, he made straight for the clubhouse. From here, the *Tribune* reported it best:

> ... He had nearly reached the gate leading from the diamond under the grand stand when someone hurled a cushion at him. It went wide of its mark, and struck a policeman instead.
>
> This was the signal for a rush. Between 300 and 400 men left their seats and started after him. Someone threw a stone which struck him in the back of the neck. A dozen policemen followed him on his way out. Thus guarded he walked to the club–house. He changed his uniform and waited a few moments until the crowd had thinned out. Then he reappeared and walked leisurely toward the entrance. As he appeared at the gate someone shouted "Fire away, boys," and at the same time started toward Woodward Avenue. The crowd, thinking that Powers had gone in that direction, hurried off. They soon learned that they had been deceived and started to follow the umpire's carriage. Stones were procured from street excavations and the mob in brutal frenzy swore vengeance upon the umpire. The carriage was impeded in its course and was

made the target for a fusillade of small stones and gravel, none of which, fortunately, did any damage.

As the umpire's carriage passed a grocery store a crowd of angry men attacked it with eggs, which were procured from the store, but the missiles fell short of the mark.

By this time there was great excitement in the street, and the driver turned off the avenue and took his charge home as rapidly as possible. Powers' head bore a big lump on the back where he had been struck by a stone as he was leaving the ground, and he was very pale and considerably agitated. Powers did not stop at the hotel tonight, but went to a friend's house. The Chicago players came in for a share of the trouble, but the element that engaged in the difficulty with them was made up largely of toughs. When the carriages were passing some one threw a stone into the carriage containing Kelly and Burns. It struck Kelly and hurt him, and the mob jeered. Others stones were thrown, but did not strike anyone. Kelly, without hesitating an instant, jumped from the carriage and started for the person who threw the stone. As Kelly stepped to the ground a burly fellow struck the Chicago rightfielder a stunning blow with his fist, knocking him down. Burns came to Kelly's aid and was hit over the head, but, being handy with his fists, made it interesting for the assailants. The man who first struck Kelly took to his heels, Kelly following. After a hot chase for a short distance Kelly laid violent hands on the fellow, and proceeded to wipe the earth with him. The fellow, it is said, was one of the party from Toledo, who were more or less intoxicated. His companion tourists rallied to his support, and the fight became general. Burns' thumb was dislocated in the row. The threatening weather had caused nearly everybody to go to the park with an umbrella, and these were now clubbed and used with considerable effect. Heads were hit right and left in the endeavor to strike the Chicago players. Burns and Kelly stood up masterfully, and did not retreat until they had caught their particular man and the instigator of the small riot and chastised him as so deserved. Ryan was attacked in his carriage and jerked out. As he went out he grabbed the horsewhip, and, regaining his perpendicular, laid about him with his whip with such effect that he soon had a circle of some feet. A number of policemen had by this time arrived on the scene and order was soon restored. The excitement created, however, did not die out for an hour. The Chicago lads finally resumed their seats in the carriages and were driven to the Russell House without further disturbance.

The attack on the players was simply an outgrowth of the bitter feeling against Powers.

The Detroit management stated that Powers caused the riot with his decision to call Burns safe in the seventh. Anson even admitted that Burns was probably out. Detroiters were quite apologetic about the incident, but they were also quick to point out that the instigators were from Toledo. However, the outcome of the game stood, and the White Stockings were now six and a half games ahead of the Wolverines with 18 days left in the season. But all was not lost for Detroit just yet as the Wolverines won the final game of the set, 6–2.

From Michigan, the Whites traveled to Philadelphia to take on the Quakers. Still barely alive in the pennant race, the Phillies pounded the White Stockings three out of four games with the odd game ending in a tie. In the meantime, Detroit swept a pair of contests from Boston to close the gap between the two frontrunners to just three games.

The Whites went to Washington next to take on the hapless Nationals. Flynn won the first game, 2–1, in seven innings, and Clarkson was the winning pitcher of the second, 8–4. McCormick made it a clean sweep, 5–4, in another seven–inning affair.

At this same time, the pennant race was being narrowed down to two teams. St. Louis dumped Philadelphia to eliminate the Phillies from contention, while New York stayed alive through September, beating the Wolverines on the last day of the month, only to be knocked out on the first of October by Detroit.

When the White Stockings arrived in New York to begin the last week of the '86 season, they held a four-game lead over Detroit and their magic number was down to six. The Giants put up a good struggle in the first game but lost to Chicago, 9–7. New York came back to win the next two games to take the series as a consolation. Detroit swept four straight from Washington to cut Chicago's lead to two and a half games, but the Whites' magic number was reduced to five with three days left in the regular season and a make–up day on

Monday, if needed.*

The Whites finished the season with a set of three games in Boston. They won the first, 8–4, then lost the second, 7–0, when Hoss Radbourne twirled a masterpiece over them. Meanwhile, Detroit played the Phillies to a tie, then beat the Quakers to close the gap to two games again.

When the sun rose on the final Saturday of the campaign, Chicago needed a win over the Beantowners and a doubleheader loss by Detroit in order to cop their second straight pennant, fifth in seven years, and sixth in the 11–year history of the National League. Clarkson stepped into the pitcher's box and held Boston to three runs in a game that was called after seven innings because of darkness, while his teammates put 12 markers on their side of the ledger.

While the White Stockings were doing their part to win the flag, Philadelphia was doing its best to keep Detroit from snatching the pennant from Chicago. The Phillies swept their twinbill with the Wolverines and made playing on Monday senseless.

When the sun set on October 9, 1886, the Chicago White Stockings were the winners of the National League title again. Proud of his team, Spalding telegraphed Anson and the boys to congratulate them:

A.C. ANSON, CAPTAIN, CHICAGO
BASE–BALL CLUB, UNITED STATES

* By League rules, the season officially ended on October 10 each year, unless that date fell on a Sunday, which it did in 1886. This gave the Wolverines one extra day to make up any games that had been cancelled earlier in the season.

HOTEL, BOSTON: *You have clinched the pennant in great style. Knew we could depend upon the old warhorses on a pinch. You have won the League championship; now come home and win the world's championship. As a token of my appreciation of your work I here-with tender each man of the team a suit of clothes and the team collectively one-half the receipts in the coming series with St. Louis. Accept my hearty congratulations.*

Spalding and Chris von der Ahe, the owner of the St. Louis Browns, had been dickering for several weeks over how they planned to play the post-season series between their champion teams. The previous attempt at playoffs had been something of a disaster with both teams claiming victory. Part of the difficulty with the '85 series stemmed from the Browns playing a St. Louis "city series" with the Maroons in the middle of the series with the White Stockings. That wouldn't be a problem in '86. The winner this year would be the first team to win four games.

As he stated in the telegram to Anson in Boston, for winning the pennant, Spalding gave each man a new suit of clothes and offered to give the players half of the gate receipts from the St. Louis series. The owner's generosity was unusual but twofold: It was an incentive for the team to win the series, and it was payment to get them to play. For this largesse, Spalding fully expected the White Stockings to win. They didn't.

The first three games were scheduled to be played in Chicago at West Side Park. Clarkson pitched the opener and shut out the Browns, 6–0. Bob Caruthers returned the favor the next day, whitewashing Chicago, 12–0, with

Tip O'Neill banging out a pair of homers. Kelly and Gore homered in the third contest, and Clarkson did his part as the Whites won, 11–4, to take a one–game lead into St. Louis.

Dave Foutz beat the White Stockings, 8–5, in the Missouri opener to even the series, then Nat Hudson moved the Browns a game up as they pounded the Whites, 10–3, in the fifth game. Clarkson had a shutout going through seven innings in Game 6, and Chicago was on top of St. Louis, 3–0. Then disaster struck in the eighth. Tommy Burns booted a ground ball that led to one run scoring, then Dalrymple misjudged a fly that let in two more. Clarkson put the final nail in the coffin lid when he wild–pitched the winning run across the plate in the bottom of the 10th. St. Louis had defeated the NL champs and now sat atop the world of professional baseball.

Rumors were in great abundance the day after the series ended. The most frequently spoken gossip was the line about Burns and Dalrymple throwing the last game; Burns because he was disgruntled over being left off Chicago's reserved player list and Dalrymple because he was mad at Anson. There was no truth to either of these stories. Burns was surprised that Spalding and Anson had kept his name off the list, but he was grateful for the opportunity to shop his talents around the League and the AA. Dalrymple may have been disgruntled, but he wasn't so angry that he would let down his teammates.

Spalding was another story. He was furious, and he let it be known to the press. Something would be done about the loss of the series to St. Louis, but he wasn't saying what — yet.

Summary

Losing the series to the St. Louis Browns was almost as disastrous to Chicago baseball fortunes as *The Great Chicago Fire* had been. At least, one would have thought so from the reactions in the newspapers and at the Chicago Board of Trade.

Chicago's baseball kranks should have looked back over the past two decades and realized that their fair city had enjoyed more success on the diamond than any other, including Boston and St. Louis. Undoubtedly, Boston sported the best teams in the '70s as the Red Stockings won four straight National Association championships and two National League flags in that decade and another in the next, and St. Louis, with the Browns, was the best of the American Association in the '80s. Even when Boston wasn't winning titles, the team was usually finishing close to the top or was at least competitive. The Browns reeled off four straight crowns in the AA and survived the challenge of Henry Lucas and the NL. But for the total years since the War Between the States, Chicago had possessed the winningest teams in all of professional baseball.

Beginning with the old Excelsior club in '65 thru '67, Chicago reigned in the West. Then the first edition of White Stockings ruled over the national scene in '70. Al

Spalding and his teammates made the Whites the domi-
nant team in the NL's inaugural season of '76. Cap
Anson put the crowning jewel on it all when he led five of
his eight teams to first place finishes in the League from
'79 thru '86. Even in the years when they weren't winning
the title, Anson's nines were more than competitive,
finishing at least 12 games over .500 in each of those
campaigns.

Such success spoiled Chicagoans just as the winning
ways of the Excelsiors back in the '60s had spoiled them
to the point that, when their favorites fell from grace,
they totally deserted the club, leaving the grandstands
devoid of patrons and thus the organization bereft of
funds to continue to support the team. The Excelsiors
seldom lost a game, which made their supporters —
mostly gamblers, pro or otherwise — winners as well.
Chicagoans took pride in their champion nine. But when
the team proved inadequate against an eastern squad —
the National Club of Washington which was made up of
government "clerks" that were allegedly hired to do
paperwork first and play baseball second — fans in the
Garden City turned on the Excelsiors with the ven-
geance of a woman betrayed by an unfaithful husband.
The club's managers hung their heads in shame and did
the honorable thing; they folded the organization.

The original stockholders of the club that succeeded
the Excelsior club were the backbone of Chicago society
and in fact were also a very large part of the original
membership of the famed Chicago Club, a men's organization that was begun shortly after the Chicago Base
Ball Club was founded. Although some of these men,
such as Potter Palmer, were sports themselves, most
were sportsmen; the difference being a sport gambled
and played the games quite seriously while a sportsman

played at the games and supported others in athletic endeavors, either directly with funds or indirectly by buying tickets to their contests. Above all, these men were Chicago's business elite, and they knew that for them to continue to make incredible sums of money off the people of Chicago and to keep Chicago growing, the people of Chicago had to have a winning attitude and that meant having a winning baseball team for them to be proud of. At the insistence of such community pro-moters as Joe Medill who was prodded by the number one baseball enthusiast on his staff, Lewis Meacham, these wealthy men banded together and formed the organization that was to last technically only six years but which actually continued to survive into the next century and beyond.

The Chicago Base Ball Club lived through *The Great Chicago Fire* as a legal entity, and it managed to remain intact through the schism of '73 when the club's mem-bership was divided over whether to field a team that year or just rent out the playing field in order to raise money for operating a nine in '74. The club was given new vigor first by Norman Gassette, then by Fred Gage and Bill Hulbert. When Gage passed away, Hulbert took full control of the club, and through a not so admirable piece of wheeling-and-dealing, he gained majority ownership for himself, effectively putting an end to the organization in the form of a club and turning it into a stock company. On Hulbert's death, ownership of the company was acquired by Al Spalding.

Through all this, players came and went, beginning with the first man to don a Chicago uniform, Jimmy Wood. Besides being the first Chicago Cub (nee White Stockings), Woodsey was also the team's first field marshal, although he bore the title of captain instead of manager. Woodsey later became the business magnate of the club, bearing the title of manager, like the manager of a prize fighter would, instead of general manager as the front office men of later years would be known.

The man who brought Woodsey to Chicago was that renowned sport, billiards player *par excellence*, gambler, saloon owner, and sound businessman, Tom Foley. He was the first victim of Chicago cleaning up its baseball act when he was shunted into relative obscurity after *The Great Chicago Fire* because of his continued association with other gamblers and various infamous members of Chicago's underworld. Foley's informal dismissal from the club was done at the instigation of the new leaders of the organization whose morality was offended by gambling and beer drinking, especially on Sundays. A few other factors leading to Foley's demise with the organization were his nationality and his politics; he was born in Ireland and was a Democrat.

At that point in Chicago's history, there was a malignancy growing within the wealthy class that thrived on a fear of foreign–born people, whether they were Irish, German, Polish, or Scandinavian. Also, the Republican Party was in control of political matters and had been since before the War Between the States. During the Civil War, many Chicago Irish Democrats were openly sympathetic to the Confederacy, and some were even implicated in the '64 conspiracy to free Confederate prisoners–of–war being detained at Fort Dearborn. For such seditious feelings and acts, the Republicans, who counted among their leaders one Joe Medill, held all Irish Democrats accountable. When the chasm between rich and poor grew greater, so did the cleft between native–born and foreign–born, and caught in the rift was Tom Foley.

Leading the new moral majority, to use a moniker coined in the 20th century, was William Ambrose Hulbert. Although not exactly a teetotaler himself, Hulbert opposed the selling of beer and liquor at the ball park for a number of reasons, and he was also against the playing of games on Sundays. Besides the obvious religious reasons for his opposition, Hulbert, like Medill and the rest of the wealthy class, associated beer-drinking with the largely foreign–born working rabble, which they saw as mostly German and Irish. Hulbert also set the price of admission to a game at 50 cents because he knew this same rabble couldn't afford many tickets at that price. As for Sunday games, he said it was wrong to play on the sabbath, but the reality of his prejudice was that Sunday was the only day the working classes had free. Hulbert was no religious zealot, but he was a man of his time, place, and station in life. The wealthy, American–born people of 1870s and 1880s Chicago distrusted and detested the poor, foreign–born working class, and William Ambrose Hulbert epitomized this fact through his handling of the Chicago White Stockings and through the formation of the National League just as much as Joe Medill did through his editorials in the *Tribune*.

When Hulbert passed from the scene, Spalding con–tinued all the practices begun by his mentor, although possibly not for the exact same reasons. Like many other wealthy Chicagoans, Spalding was the first in his family to strike it rich in the booming city, but unlike many of the rest, he was a Westerner by birth, not a New England Yankee, New Yorker, or Pennsylvanian who had come west to find or gouge his fortune out of the burgeoning Illinois metropolis. Like Marshall Field, Spalding came from farm folk, and also like Field, he worked his way up through the ranks until he had earned a great fortune. But unlike Field and much of the rest of the social elite, Spalding *acquired* his prejudice through his desire to please his great benefactor, Bill Hulbert, and through his desire to become an integral part of Chicago's upper social strata and its business community. When Hulbert died and Spalding took his place, there was no great immediate change in the manner in which the Chicago White Stockings baseball team was operated. A rather smooth transition took place, and life went on. Spalding did gradually become his own man, and when he did, he became self-destructive.

However, that story must be reserved for another time.

For now, the initial portion of the history of the Chicago Cubs must be concluded because the organization and the team were on the verge of mutating, which is a story in itself.

Conclusion

O for those simpler days again! when fans were called kranks and when someone yelled, "Kill the umpire!" everyone looked around for the guy with a rope.

The pace of life was so much slower in the 19th Century. Horses and carriages instead of automobiles; trains that raced along at 30 miles per hour instead of subsonic jet aircraft streaking across the sky. Folks walked almost everywhere in the cities and towns; unlike modern people who drive three blocks to the corner convenience store to pick up a loaf of bread and a quart of oil. What an easy–going time it was!

And as a Cubs fan, I really miss those years between 1869 and 1887. What a glorious time to root for the hometown team! So what if they were called the White Stockings or Whites or White Socs or White Socks? They were still Chicago's team. And more than that, they were winners. Year after year, they were in the race for the whip flag. And they won the pennant six times in the National League's first 11 years, not to mention being unofficial champs in 1870. I'll slide on the 1871 season. No use crying over spilled milk. We Cubs fans know who was the real champion that year, and that's all that counts.

Yes, those were the days all right. Glorious days!

While reading the old books and the newspapers of the time, my imagination often carried me back to those times, and I would see myself sitting in the grandstand at Union Grounds or the park at 23rd and State streets. Anson would be playing first base, Pfeffer second, Williamson third, Burns at short, Dalrymple in left, Gore in center, and Kelly in right with Flint behind the plate and John Clarkson on the hill. Clarkson would whirl and twirl and whip the ball across the plate, and Flint would catch it with his bare hands and whip it back to Clarkson before the ump could say strike three. The crowd would come to its feet and roar with approval as big Dan Brouthers, the fiercest hitter of the time, stepped sullenly back to the visitors bench. Clarkson would whiff the next two hitters and the inning would be over; time for the home team to take the bat. Burns would lead off and bounce a single through the hole between short and third into left. Gore would follow with a solid liner into center, and up would step the captain and manager of the team, Adrian Anson. He was the biggest man in the game, and he was a big man, standing over six feet tall and weighing better than 200 pounds. Cap Anse would slug the ball deep into the gap between left and center, and like gazelles, Burns and Gore would race around the bases to score easily. And the rally was on!

And when my imagination wasn't working so well, my memory would never fail me. I would recall the first time I ever saw the Cubs in the flesh.

It was Spring Training 1960, and the Cubs were in Scottsdale, Arizona to play the Boston Red Sox. My dad took my best friend Tracy Ford and me to the game. It was a Sunday and the wooden stadium was packed so full that we had to stand along the short fence between the backstop screen and the Red Sox's dugout. Ron Santo played third base that day, and we were so close to him that I could almost touch him. What a day! I saw Ernie Banks, my number one hero. Billy Williams was a rookie in the outfield, and Dale Long hit two homers. The Cubs lost in a typical early spring shootout, but I didn't care. I got to see my Cubs. I got to see Ted Williams, too, but that wasn't a big deal then — at least not for a 13-year-old.

Oddly, the first time I was supposed to see the Cubs in Wrigley Field was on a Saturday in 1957. The Pirates were in town. So was Jane Russell. So was the rain. No game. Darn! Dad wasn't buying any tickets until he was sure the game was on, so the closest my brothers and I — all of us Cubs fans — got to getting inside to see those ivy-covered walls was the ticket booth at the main gate. But I did see Cal Neeman and another Cub whose number I didn't get. Maybe I shouldn't say oddly considering that the Cubs first scheduled night game at Wrigley Field was rained out. Is that kismet or something like that? Na-a-ah! I guess not.

The next time I went to Wrigley Field I got in. It was the second game of the season 1969. The Phillies were in Chicago. The Cubs creamed them, 10–0, behind Bill Hands. I was a little kid again. I figured the Cubs would win it all that year because I had finally gotten to Wrigley Field to see the Cubs play.

We all know what happened in '69. I guess I wasn't the catalyst that would make them the champs. I wonder how many other fans felt like me, that they were the lucky charm for the Cubs that year only to have their hearts broken in September.

And how about some of the years since then?

As much as I hate to admit it, we fans are not the lucky charms for the Cubs. No, we're a fringe benefit. Solid management in the front office and on the field is what it takes to make the Cubs a winner.

Which brings me back to this book. The Chicago club had that solid management, and Chicago had a winner. That goes to show that winning — in any business — begins at the top. I thought the Cubs were headed back to that when Dallas Green came to Chicago. It's too early to tell whether he started something new or not. Only time will tell. Until history does pass judgment on the Green Era, I guess I'll have to hold on to the past and try to relive those hallowed days when the Cubs were the White Sox.

BIBLIOGRAPHY

Ahrens, Art & Gold, Eddie; *Day by Day in Chicago Cubs History;* New York Leisure Press; 1982

Akin, William E.; An Article: *Barehands and Kid Gloves: The Best Fielders, 1880–1899;* Baseball Research Journal; 1981; pages 60–65.

Allen, Lee; *The National League;* New York; Hill & Wang: 1961

Anson, Adrian Constantine; *A Ball Player's Career;* Chicago; Era Publishing Co.; 1900

Barry, Henry & Cook, Bob; *A Baseball Century;* New York; Macmillan; 1976

Bartlett, Arthur Charles; *Baseball and Mr. Spalding;* New York; Farrar, Straus & Young; 1951

Brown, Gene; *The Complete Book of Baseball;* New York; Arno Press; Indianapolis; Bobbs–Merrill; 1980

Brown, Warren; *The Chicago Cubs;* New York; G.P. Putnam's Sons; 1946

Chicago Historical Society; Chicago Cubs Collection: Box 1 — pages 1–12 pages 50–55 pages 287 — 292. — Box 4 — pages 2–7 ledger page 7 pages 9–11.

Chicago *Journal* Newspapers; Assorted Copies

Chicago *Tribune* Newspapers; Assorted copies

Chicago *Times* Newspapers; Assorted copies

Couzins, Gerald Secor; *A Baseball Album;* New York; Lippincott & Crowell; 1980

Durso, Joseph; *Baseball and the American Dream;* St. Louis; The Sporting News; 1986

Enright, Jim; *Chicago Cubs;* New York; Macmillian; 1975

Frommer, Harvey; *Primitive Baseball;* New York; Antheneum; 1988

Gold, Eddie & Ahrens, Art; *The Golden Era Cubs 1876–1945*; Chicago; Bonus Books; 1985

Gold, Eddie; An Article: *Hall Would Be Home for Hulbert*; Baseball Research Journal; 1981; pages 99–101.

Honig, Donald: *Baseball America*; New York; Macmillan; 1985

James, Bill; *The Bill James Historical Baseball Abstract*; New York; Villard Books; 1986

Lange, Fred W.; *History of Baseball in California and Pacific Coast Leagues, 1847–1938*; Oakland, CA; 1938

Leitner, Irving A.; *Baseball: Diamond in the Rough*; New York; Criterion; 1972

Levine, Peter; *A. G. Spalding and the Rise of Baseball*; New York; Oxford University Press; 1985

Morse, Jacob; *Sphere & Ash: History of Baseball 1888*; Columbia, SC; Camden House 1984

Muhlbach, Robert; An Article: *Billy Sunday, Evangelist*; Baseball Research Journal; pages 5–7.

Murdock, Eugene C.; An Article: *The Pre–1900 Batting Stars*; Baseball Research Journal; pages 75–78.

New York *Evening Post* Newspapers; Various Articles

New York *Herald* Newspapers; Various Articles

New York *Sun* Newspapers; Various Articles

New York *Times* Newspapers; Various Articles

New York *Tribune* Newspapers; Various Articles

Okrent, Daniel & Lewine, Harris; *The Ultimate Baseball Book*; New York: Houghton Mifflin Company: 1979

Orem, Preston D.; *Baseball 1845–1881*; Altadena, CA; 1961

Phillips, David R.; *That Old Ball Game*; Chicago; Regnery; 1975

Reichler, Joseph; *The Baseball Encyclopedia*; New York; Macmillian; 1985

Riess, Steven A.; *Touching Base*; Westport, Connecticut;

Greenwood Press; 1980

Ritter, Lawrence S.; *The Glory of Their Times*; New York; Vintage Books; 1966

Ritter, Lawrence S.; *The Image of Greatness*; New York; Crown; 1979

Seymour, Harold; *Baseball*; New York, Oxford University Press; 1960.

Shannon, Bill; *The Ball Parks*; New York; Hawthorn; 1975

Smith, Robert Miller; *Baseball in America*; New York; Holt, Rinehart & Winston; 1961

Society for American Baseball Researchers; *The National Pastime*; Cooprerstown, New York; Spring 1984

Spalding, Albert Goodwill; *Albert Goodwill Spalding 1850–1915*; New York; American Sports Publishing; 1911

Spalding, A.G.; *America's National Game*; New York; American Sports Publishing; 1911

Spink, Alfred Henry; *The National Game*; St. Louis; The National Game Publishing Co.; 1910

Tattersall, John C.; An Article: *Clarifying An Early Home Run Record*; Baseball Research Journal; pages 10–18.

The Sporting News Newspapers; Various Articles

Voigt, David Quentin; *American Baseball*; University of Oklahoma Press; 1966

Voigt, David Quentin; *Baseball, An Illustrated History*; Pennsylvania State University; 1987

Index

–H–

–K–

–L–

–M–

–N–

Acknowledgements

I cannot tell a lie. I did not do all the work that went into this book. Not all by myself, anyway. I had help. Lots of it.

Craig Cramer and his staff at the Wisconsin State Historical Society Microfilm Section pitched in and helped me find just a few reels of microfilm from which I read several thousand pages of fuzzy six–point type detailing events as they happened and were reported by the Chicago *Tribune* and other newspapers of the 19th Century. Thanks, Craig and crew.

Another thankyou goes to the Chicago Historical Society, specifically Clarence Clark for assisting me in finding just the right papers that he and the CHS preserve so preciously. These guardians of Chicago's past deserve much more appreciation than I'm sure they receive.

She'd say that she didn't do all that much, but every little bit helps. She is my sister–in–law Ann Eagan, and now she can give new meaning to the title: "What I Did on My Summer Vacation." Thanks, Annetha.

A grudging thanks goes to Gregory Kenneth for applying the turtle wax at most of the right places.

Thanks also to my son Tory for letting Dad work when both of us would have preferred to be in the woods hunting or at the lake fishing.

But more than all the others combined, I thank my wife Peggy who isn't really very fond of baseball but who is my Number One research assistant whether the subject is baseball, football, or the Old West. Besides finding many of the sources of information used in this book, she also had to listen to me talk baseball well into most nights. Fortunately, she has a friend whose better half is worse than I when it comes to lecturing his lady on the game. He gives quizzes — and in front of friends, too. Ain't love grand?

Bury My Heart at Wrigley Field

Other books by Larry D. Names

The Shaman's Secret

Twice Dead

The Legend of Eagle Claw

Bose

Boomtown

The Cowboy Conspiracy

The History of the Green Bay Packers:
The Lambeau Years – Part One

The History of the Green Bay Packers:
The Lambeau Years – Part Two